PARENTING TEENAGERS

By the time we get the hang of parenting, our children have left home! Most of us have had to learn parenting through the school of hard-knocks. But isn't it wiser to learn from others? Thank God for this book – it will amuse, motivate, inspire and equip. We wish we'd been able to read this before we started parenting our teenagers!

Killy and J John
Philo Trust

An ever-increasing number of parents are desperate to find material that will encourage and inspire them as they rise to the challenge of bringing up their teenagers. This book is enjoyable, straightforward, balanced and biblical. Paul and Christine have a proven track record of bringing up their own teenagers, and we would highly recommend every parent with teenagers in the home to get hold of this book.

Mark and Karen Bailey
Holy Trinity, Cheltenham

Realistic, manageable, easy to follow and constantly referring to 'the Bible view' – this course will be a God-send to many parents who are bringing up teenage children and feel they could do the job a little better! As the parents of five children, three of them teenagers, we are so grateful to draw on Paul and Christine's Bible knowledge, wisdom and experience.

Andrew and Katherine Cornes
All Saints, Crowborough

We at New Wine have always valued our young people and so we are thrilled that Paul and Christine have provided, at our invitation, a *Family Time* sequel. Every church wanting to help teenagers and their parents needs to have this resource among its family life courses.

John and Anne Coles
New Wine

We enthusiastically recommend this book for anyone who has anything to do with the wonderful world of teenagers! It covers the whole gamut of issues facing parents with honesty, wit and wisdom, offering invaluable help that is both practical and biblical.

Lyndon and Celia Bowring
Care

Parenting Teenagers

Family Time

Paul and Christine Perkin

Published by David C. Cook
Kingsway Communications Ltd
26–28 Lottbridge Drove, Eastbourne BN23 6NT, UK

David C. Cook
4050 Lee Vance View, Colorado Springs, CO 80918, USA

David C. Cook Distribution Canada
55 Woodslee Avenue, Paris, Ontario, Canada N3L 3E5

ISBN 978 1 84291 379 6

First published 2008
1 2 3 4 5 6 7 Printing / Year 11 10 09 08

Cover design: PinnacleCreative.co.uk
Printed in Great Britain

Contents

Acknowledgements

We want to thank our three children – Emily, Julia and Max – who have bravely allowed their stories to be used, and who have vetted their transmission along the way! They still haven't decided whether to be amused or horrified that we've been writing this material on parenting teenagers, but they have given their permission for every example and illustration we use from our experience of family life. In that sense we feel this is a real joint venture and we want to thank them for their willingness to share their misdemeanours and canny insights with so many others.

We're so grateful to our wonderful congregation at St Mark's, who have helped and encouraged us as we've worked on this material over the last few years.

We want to thank Mark and Lindsay Melluish for the privilege of being entrusted with the sequel to their *Family Time – Parenting Children*. It's been such fun working with them.

Thank you also to Nicky and Sila Lee and Rob and Di Parsons, who have promoted family life in our nation and given fresh hope and resources to so many people. They have all been such a personal inspiration to us.

Preface

This book is based on a set of talks we put together as a *Parenting Teenagers* course for our church, St Mark's Battersea Rise in London. Mark and Lindsay Melluish then invited us to contribute this material as a sequel to their *Parenting Children* course and book, and unite them both under the 'Family Time' banner.

You may want simply to read this book for yourself in your parenting, or you may see how this material could help you to run a parenting course in your own locality. It's one thing to read a book about parenting on your own, but we feel there is an enormous amount to be gained by learning and sharing experiences with other parents.

Through these teenage years parents easily become isolated from each other when there is no more standing together at the school gate or collecting children from each other's homes. For this reason alone we feel there is something very significant about parents attending a course together – it's a wonderful opportunity for parents to connect with other parents facing similar issues and for ongoing friendship and support.

With this in mind we have included an appendix at the end of the book entitled 'How to Run a *Parenting Teenagers* Course', which gives details of how to run a course of your own.

Introduction

'It was the best of times, it was the worst of times.' The opening sentence of Charles Dickens' *A Tale of Two Cities* could be the catch-phrase of many parents to describe life with teenagers in the home! These years can be some of the happiest and some of the hardest of a family's life. Most parents feel that they move into completely new territory when their children hit the teenage years.

How do we view the teenage years: with dread or expectation? Many of us, if we're honest, are led to anticipate the worst. We've heard enough stories from parents who've gone ahead of us, and they've filled us with apprehension. Why is it we always remember the nightmare scenarios?

The fact is that these teenage years are going to be different – different from what we've known of family life so far – and that can be unnerving for us as parents. Even the word 'teenager' implies that we're heading into unusual territory. The teenage years are the 'in-between' years – no longer a child but not yet an adult – and that may feel uncomfortable, for us and for them.

Actually the word 'teenager' wasn't used until the mid-1900s. Before then, people were thought of in just two stages: children and adults. At age 13 or 14 a girl became a woman, a boy became a man; and at that point they were ready to do adult work. It was as simple and significant as that.

But the reforms of the early twentieth century, preventing child labour and ensuring secondary education, lengthened the pre-adult years. Now, while adult size was achieved as soon as ever, preparation for adult responsibilities lasted until age 18 or later. The years ending in 'teen' became something new and distinctive.

These years were either to be enjoyed as 'the best of times', combining childhood freedom with adult physical maturity; or endured as 'the worst of times', combining childish irresponsibility with adult urges; or most likely a combination of the two!

In our experience they have certainly been rollercoaster years. We have had moments of high tension, of great pride, of extreme anxiety and of enormous fun – sometimes all in just one day! But in amongst it all our teenagers have become great companions and tremendous catalysts, as they have stimulated ideas and shared questions and aspirations.

Contrary to media hype, most teenagers pass through their teenage years relatively trouble-free. Research shows that nearly 60 per cent of young people said they 'get on well with their parents'. In this book we want to dare to say that these teenage years are not merely to be survived but are years of hope and opportunity – for us in our parenting as well as for our teenagers. This is the time to connect with our child as never before.

In these chapters we are going to take a look at a number of different areas of life with teenagers in the house. We want to offer some practical suggestions and observations, and in each chapter we include points where we encourage you to 'Stop & Think' through some of the practical outworkings of the issues raised. As you read this book we would encourage you to use the material in it to open up lines of communication with your teenagers. Ask them what they think. Find out if they agree with what's being said. If you're doing the course, then the course handbook will help you with this and provides exercises to enable you to work through the topics raised.

We end each chapter with some typical scenes from teenage life for you to think through. These scenes will relate to some aspect of the topics covered in that chapter, and will help you to think through the practical outworkings of the issues. There is also a section called 'Taking It Further', which suggests some tasks to put into practice in your family. We include these suggestions because we believe that there is real value in putting things into action straight away, and we would strongly encourage you to take on these tasks as you read the book. The truth is, we will all have much more chance of effecting real change in our family's life and in our relationships if we don't just read about things but do them as well!

We believe that this book will tell us as much about ourselves as it will about our teenagers, and that it will give us an opportunity to take a fresh look at our parenting – at the relationship we have built with our children and how we can help that to grow.

Chapter 1

A GALAXY FAR, FAR AWAY

The Teenage Universe

PARALLEL UNIVERSES

Our teenager's world and our own world often seem far apart.

UNDERSTANDING OUR WORLD AND THEIRS

'Children are tyrants. They contradict their parents, gobble their food and tyrannise their teachers.' So said Socrates, back in ancient Greece – nothing much seems to have changed!

Our world

We all parent very differently. We come from different backgrounds and experiences. We have different hopes and expectations, different values and priorities. We may have made very different homes: some will be single, widowed, separated, divorced, or remarried. These factors will all affect the kind of home that we are building.

Step-parents and single parents

Step-families and single-parent families face many significant pressures. It's beyond the scope of this book to give particular focus to these families, and in any case the majority of the issues we face as parents of teenagers raise the same questions and need the same handling whatever our situation. But here are just a few words on step-families and single-parent families, as these have increasing significance for parenting in the twenty-first century.

It's predicted that in a few years there will be more children living in a step-family than in a biological or traditional family. If teenage life in a traditional family is complicated, in a step-family, where there will be some relationships with no blood ties or shared history, it can be even more so. A teenager may well come into the step-family bringing sad, unhealthy or even traumatic previous experiences. These may include hurt, death, rejection or betrayal.

Relationships between step-parent and child take time to build, and if they're trying to establish these relationships during their family's teenage years, it can often be particularly hard. An older child may well have subconsciously taken on a very adult role in the absence of a parent, and may easily feel threatened by the arrival of a new partner.

Step-parents often say that they feel they have many responsibilities but no rights; and a hurting teenager will quickly learn to play on this dilemma – hence the 'wicked step-mother' scenario in many step-families.

Combining two sets of children, sometimes of very different ages, is likely to be a challenge. Here is a glimpse of one step-mother's experience: 'When my husband's teenagers come to stay, my six-year-old daughter sees them as here to play, but teenagers don't "play"! We've worked hard at balancing their need for space and our need to have them as part of the family.'

For single parents, relationships with their teenagers can become particularly intense. The burden of responsibility is very heavy. It's hard enough for two parents working together to remain strong, but understandably it is harder when all the decisions, discipline and care has to come from just one person.

Discipline is a particularly difficult area. Although the words 'I'll tell your father' are probably not heard in many homes today, when you're feeling low or tired it can be a comforting thought that reinforcements are on the way at the end of the day. Someone to come in and say, 'Your mother is right, and you're grounded, and turn off the TV *now*!'

The day-to-day parent can often feel like the 'bad guy'. A familiar scenario is that of a parent with custody struggling on a tight budget and the other parent with occasional access spending lavishly on the children. This is especially hard if earlier requests from the children for meals out or other treats have been declined, and then they return home from access visits with DVDs or tales of a 'fantastic day out'.

One single mother says: 'I was pleased for the kids to have a good time, but I could weep over the money spent on unessential things. I would love to spoil them too, sometimes, but from me they hear a "No, I can't buy you that at the moment".'

We are aware that we may not be addressing many of the specific issues relating to single or step-parents, but we hope that you will find real strength and encouragement from this book as you face parenting through the teenage years.

It's important (and useful) as we begin to look at our own parenting to understand first what sort of person we are. What is important to us?

Stop & Think

Can you answer the following questions about yourself?

- What sort of personality do you have?
  (easy-going, ambitious, perfectionist, pessimistic. . .)
- What sort of home do you think you run?
  (permissive, strict, easy-going. . .)
- What particularly pressurises you?
  (work, money, health, relationships. . .)
- What is important to you in life?
  (education, sport, lifestyle, religious faith. . .)
- What or who most influences you?
  (peer group, spouse, your own parents. . .)

Another useful exercise is to try to remember your own teenage years and experiences, because remembering how it was for you as a teenager will enable you to relate more effectively to your own adolescents. We're made to believe that the teenage world is very different now from our day and that we won't understand the issues they're facing, but actually the emotions and growing pains are very similar.

Thinking about how you felt at that age, and remembering how you handled issues, can be a good starting point for relating to your own teenagers. You'll be surprised by how many memories come flooding in once you start allowing yourself to think back.

Stop & Think

Try to remember back to when you were 14 or 15 years old and answer the following questions:

- Whose opinion mattered most in all the world to you?
- Can you name three friends whose homes you liked going to? Why did you like these in particular?
- Do you remember the first boy/girl you were attracted to?
- What annoyed you most about your parents? Can you remember specific things they said or did that embarrassed you?
- What 'idols' did you have through your teenage years? Was there a pop group, film star or football team that you were besotted with?
- Can you name three things that were sacrosanct in your family when you were a teenager (e.g. meals must be eaten in the kitchen or dining room, not in front of the TV)?
- Was there someone you liked who hardly seemed to even notice you? What did it feel like?
- Can you remember your parents denying you something? How did you react?

That's looking at *our* world. Now let's look at *their* world.

Their world

How well do we know their world? Keeping up with teenagers is hard work because things change so fast.

Their likes

These are constantly changing – what they like to do, what they like to wear, what they like to listen to and who they like to hang around with. These things will change from month to month, if not week to week! We need to make an effort to know about their world and share their interests – to understand their culture and the things that are important to them. It can feel like learning a foreign language sometimes, but it's worth the effort. And in among all the hard stuff, let's remind ourselves that our teenagers are great fun – they can be witty, relaxed, idealistic and tremendously stimulating. So let's enjoy their world too.

Stop & Think

Can you answer these questions about your teenager(s)?

- What are the names of their three best friends?
- What are their favourite TV programmes?
- What kind of music do they listen to – do you know the names of the artists?
- What is their latest fashion 'essential'?
- Where do they spend their evenings out – what do they do?
- Who influences their opinions most?
- What do they find difficult in their relationship with you?
- Do you know how they most recently spent more than £20?

Be aware that understanding is not necessarily 'entering into' their world. The temptation for some of us is to try to be a teenager again. We think that to get alongside them we have to show that we're still young and trendy at heart.

On a recent holiday we were playing a favourite family game one evening. It involves choosing a name, and Paul, who isn't the most clued up on pop culture, had been paying attention to the kids' conversations during the day and had picked up the name J-Lo. He thought it would impress them if he casually used the name, but unfortunately he hadn't quite picked up how to pronounce it, and called her 'J-*Low*' (putting the stress on the wrong syllable), which caused gales of laughter and simply reinforced how out of touch he was! But they love that. They love being able to tease us.

The lesson we have learned is that we don't need to be their best mates. They have lots of 'mates', but only one mum and dad. Our relationship with them is unique.

Their needs

Let's ask ourselves what kind of home we are trying to create for our family through these years. We all want to build an atmosphere in our home that encourages our teenagers to grow up in positive and healthy ways. We know that in theory, but in practice it's hard to hold on to and to keep working towards the things that are *really* important to us because day-to-day survival just takes over.

Here are a few suggestions (adapted from Nicky and Sila Lee) as to what our home needs to be for them – particularly during these teenage years. First, our home needs to be:

(a) A place to be known

Do our teenagers know that they are loved unconditionally? Can they be open and honest with us? Can they make mistakes and move on?

Our younger daughter, Julia, found the last few years at school quite a struggle and often seemed to learn lessons the hard way. The culmination was an incident at school involving a prank with four dozen eggs! One of the things she said recently was how much she valued us standing alongside her during that time. We didn't bail her out, but we didn't judge her either, and most importantly we allowed her to move on.

Second, our home needs to be:

(b) A place to grow

Are we providing a place where our teenagers can grow in confidence, so they can meet the outside world secure in who they are? Do we respect their opinions and views as they develop them?

Paul remembers vividly a holiday in Scotland that we spent with another family when our children were in their very early teens. We were all having dinner together one evening and our host started asking our children various questions. He was really interested in what our teenagers had to say, but Paul was concerned because he didn't think they would have any understanding on these particular subjects. In fact he was about to interrupt and answer on their behalf, and this man stopped him. Paul learned an important lesson that holiday: our children had opinions of their own and an ability and interest in discussing them in an adult way, and he needed to allow them to express themselves.

Do we have healthy discussions on a variety of topics? Can we disagree on issues without falling out? It's natural for teenagers to want to think things through for themselves – our word and experience as a parent is not enough any more.

Are we helping our teenagers to face disappointment? The reality of life through these years is that they're going to face failure of some kind, or feel let down; they will probably face rejection; there will be stress at school over exams; there will be pressure from their peers to conform. All these things will knock their confidence.

One of our goals should be to raise a child who can face disappointment, even failure, and not be crushed by it. Maybe that sounds a surprising goal to aim at, as we so often concentrate on raising a child who will be successful. We are so achievement-orientated that we can easily forget that some of the most important lessons in life are learned when we fail.

This means that we, as parents, should not always feel that we have to protect them from life's knocks. Our role, particularly through these teenage years, needs to be in supporting and encouraging them, especially when they fail. Rather than desperately protecting them, we need to see that even failure can be a growth point.

(c) A place to laugh

Is there teasing and easy banter? Our son Max is now a good six inches taller than Christine and he loves coming up to her and putting her under his chin and saying, 'Mummy, you're so little and so old!'

The children have also noticed that Paul is a bit of a pessimist and this would often show itself when the family was under pressure to make a deadline. For example, we would be halfway to the airport to catch a plane and we could almost guarantee that Paul would say, 'Well, that's it, we've definitely missed it now – I told you all we should have left an hour earlier. We might as well turn round and go home.' This would succeed in annoying us all!

But our teenagers have managed to turn things around by deciding at such times to say it for him before he does. So it's now become standard practice that one of them will exclaim, 'Well that's it, we've definitely missed it. We might as well go home!'

Try not to ignore the building of family traditions. In our home, for instance, for a period of time during their early teens Friday night was video night. We would rent a video and buy some big bags of popcorn, turn out all the lights, move all the sofas round to face the TV, and stay up far too late.

(d) A place to retreat

Will our teenagers find comfort when they've been hurt? Will they find support from outside pressures? Will they be listened to when they're confused?

We remember our eldest daughter, Emily, breaking up with her first boyfriend. She had only been going out with him rather sporadically for a few months, but she was distraught. And after a number of days of heart-breaking tears and endless conversations it was very tempting to say, 'Come on, darling, it's not so bad – you'll be OK.' But that's not what she needed to hear! She just needed a lot of cups of tea and sympathy.

> Bible View:
>
> The Bible tells us that the basis of a secure, fun, learning, growing and accepting home is to know our home within God's family.

> 'How great is the love the Father has lavished on us, that we should be called children of God! And that is what we are!' (1 John 3:1).
>
> We don't have to try to be God's children. By faith in him we are already members of his family, which means that nothing we can ever do will make him love us more and nothing we can ever do will make him love us less.

Stop & Think

Our homes need to be places where our teenagers can be known, where they can grow, where they can laugh, and where they can retreat to.

What kind of home are you creating? Which of these four elements are strongest? Which need some work?

EATING UP TIME

BLACK HOLES THAT EAT UP TIME

UNDERSTANDING THEIR GREATEST NEED

We all want our home to be a place of safety, fun, learning, growth and acceptance: in other words, a loving home. But what makes for this? We suggest that a key thing to think about at this point is investing our time.

Being available

This is vital during the teenage years. It's so easy to see a teenager's increasing independence as them moving *away* from the family – needing us less. So we find ourselves spending less and less time with them. Feelings of 'remoteness' and 'disconnection' grow between us. To allow this to happen is one of the most devastating mistakes parents can make today.

We must understand that children need, and often want, time with us. The older our teenagers get, the more they need us – even if they don't admit it; and that's because as they get older they face many more complex issues and dilemmas. They will be feeling pressure from all sides – friends, school, society – and they need somewhere they can take refuge. We are a significant place of refuge for them.

The writer Paul Francis says, 'They need you as a base they can return to, a sheltered harbour, so that when the storm gets rough they can head back to you.' That means we have to create time and often make it a priority above everything else.

'Being available' would be a very good motto for parents of teenagers. How available do we feel we are to our teenagers?

Bible View:

The Bible has many models of this availability. For example, Paul's estimate of his close friend Timothy is a model for all parents. He said:

'I have no-one else like him, who takes a genuine interest in your welfare' (Philippians 2:20).

The starting point of that kind of love involves spending time and thoughtfulness and energy.

Life inevitably moves on for us parents, as well as for our teenagers.

Stop & Think

How available do we feel we are to our teenagers? What makes us less available through these years?

- Are there younger siblings to look after?
- Are new career opportunities opening up?
- Are there other emotional pressures on us?
- Are social or sporting activities taking up time?

'Being available' is very hard for us as parents because we see time as such a precious commodity. But we need to be generous in the time we give them during these years, and we need to be honest with ourselves about how much time we are prepared to give our teenagers.

Being honest

We sometimes prefer to talk in terms of spending quality time with our children as opposed to quantity time, so we say things like,

'I don't have a lot of time with my kids, but the five minutes we have each day is really good quality time.'

Tim Smith, in his book *Almost Cool*, interestingly comments, 'Quality time is a myth created by adults. The concept of quality time is driven by the need of the parents, who are often over-committed and try to assign a few minutes of their hectic schedules to activities devoted to their children and call it quality time!' We need to be honest about our own situation and what we are able and prepared to give to our teenagers through these years.

One parent commented, 'The trouble is, there's an awful lot of just hanging around where teenagers are concerned!'

Being imaginative

We need to be imaginative about the ways we can spend time with our teenagers. When they were little it was so much easier; we took them to the park, or played in the garden or read a book. They *wanted* (often demanded!) us to spend time with them.

With older children it's harder, and it often seems to involve spending money! It could be taking them shopping or to a football match; taking them out for a meal or a burger or a cup of coffee. But we've certainly found that it's money well spent if it means one-on-one time with them.

If it's not the investment of money, it can simply be the time – time we'd rather spend doing something of our own choice. Life is set at such a fast pace that it's difficult to make time unless we plan it – time both with our children individually and with the family. We can have all the right intentions, but if we leave it to chance we can find that a whole month has gone by and we've hardly seen each other, let alone talked together.

Stop & Think

Think of some particularly good memories of things you've done together, either individually or as a family. What made them special? How could you recreate them without turning the clock back?

A QUESTION OF RELATIVITY

UNDERSTANDING CHANGE

We can't turn the clock back; the childhood days are now gone for ever. A revolution is taking place – in their lives and ours. Life for teenagers is unpredictable: their mood swings, their plans (or lack of them), their likes and dislikes. That makes life for us as their parents rather unpredictable too, and we can look back with longing at the straightforward 'timetabled' days of their childhood. But the pattern of family life will inevitably change as both children and parents grow and develop.

Youth pastor Daniel Hahn says this: 'Parents face two options. We can keep using the same patterns we used when they were young (and frustrate ourselves to death), or we can come to realise that our methods must change as our kids develop.'

We suggest four 'R's to help you develop some strategies to move with change rather than try to fight against it: recognise, relax, rejoice, release.

Recognise

Recognise when you have reached a time of change. Watch what is happening at the 'top end' of the family. Don't let the youngest members always dictate what everyone should do. There is a danger, if the eldest is constantly pushing the boundaries, that we will retreat to the youngest because they are more responsive. There can often be a big difference in years between our oldest child and our youngest. Be alert to the changing lifestyle patterns of teenagers.

Relax

Be gentle with yourselves and with them. The guilt that most of us batter ourselves with is the false guilt of perfectionism. There's a recording running in our head that tells us endlessly what we should do, what we failed to do and what everyone else is doing that is working so much better. And if we listen too much to the negative recording, it makes us feel defeated and discouraged. And what is worse, we begin acting out all those negative things.

So we need to beware of comparing ourselves with other families and competing with the parents. We all know there is a tendency to compete when the children are young – over their first distinguishable word, their first tottering step, their first mouthful of solids. But this all becomes more serious and damaging when we're competing over their achievements as they grow into adulthood – over their exam results, their prospects after school, their sporting successes.

We've known other parents over the years who were always wanting to compare their children's achievements with ours. Teenagers are quick to pick this up. Our children do a brilliant imitation of one particular parent who is always boasting of their children's successes. Beware!

Problems with teenagers can also hit us at a difficult time in our lives. Many of us are around 40 and reaching a mid-life crisis when our children are going through adolescence.

Charles Bradshaw, in *You and Your Teen*, says, 'The adolescent's spirit often collides with his parents' mid-life reassessment – that critical time in their life when marriage, careers, life pursuits, values and priorities are questioned, turned around and drastically altered.' Parents and teenagers face similar life-stage issues at the same time. Often, though, they are heading in different directions.

We may be feeling that life is passing us by, and that we may never realise some of our hopes and dreams. We may feel tired or even depressed at times, and want to come home to peace in the evenings – not to raised voices and blaring music.

We look at these young people who have everything ahead of them, and it may remind us of some of the opportunities we've missed.

So be aware of these different pressures and try to give yourself some space as you adjust to this new phase in your own life.

Rejoice

Enjoy who your children are now and where they have got to. Don't look back; look forward!

We may never have appreciated at the time how relatively simple the primary school years were. Life was so straightforward. Life with teenagers can feel very complicated, and when faced with this spotty, grunting, difficult child we can be tempted to look back and think, 'Where did that sweet-natured, outgoing, compliant child go?' But we must move on.

Parenting teenagers isn't about changing our teenager – it's about understanding the changes facing our teenager and helping them to work through them.

Release

Release them. Be prepared when a time of change has come to do things differently. Accept it; don't fight it! Begin to create new patterns that are right for the situation as it is now, not as it used to be.

We found that there was an extremely short space of time when our children got up in the morning at what we would call a decent hour. From the early years when they would wake us at six o'clock even at weekends (and that was a lie-in!) to spending virtually all day in bed there seemed to be about one month when our sleep patterns coincided! We decided that instead of spending most of Saturday mornings getting cross and nagging our teenagers to get out of bed and start the day, we would do brunch at eleven or twelve o'clock, and make it a fun morning instead of a battle.

Our ultimate goal at this stage in their lives should be to release them; to prepare them for independence, when they'll be making decisions for themselves.

Stop & Think

As you consider the four 'R's, how well do you feel you are working these out as your family changes around you? Is there one you could do something about right now?

TYPICAL TEENAGE SCENES

Take a look at these typical scenes from teenage life and consider what action you would take if you were faced with these situations.

1. We used to be a wonderfully close family and always did fun things together at the weekends. But now suddenly our 15-year-old son refuses to take part in any family activities. He either stays in his room with the door shut listening to music, or he goes out on his bike to meet his mates. I'm afraid that his siblings will simply follow his lead and we'll have no family time left at all. What should we do?

2. We have always spent family summer holidays together in a cottage in Devon. Our 18-year-old daughter has suddenly announced that she has made alternative plans to go with some friends to Spain. Our 16-year-old is now up in arms and says that if her sister isn't coming with us, she doesn't want to come either. What should we still expect? When do you allow them to make plans of their own?

3. I have three teenagers of 13, 14 and 16. I have just taken on a job that means I won't be home until 6 pm most evenings. I've always been there for them when they've come in from school, and I'm unsure whether this is a right move to make at this stage in their teens. What would you advise?

FOLLOW-UP QUESTIONS

- How do you hold together the 'top end' of your family with the younger members? How is your time divided between your different children?
- Do you have particular shared activities with your teenagers? How do you see these changing/developing as they get older? What new activities could you instigate?

RE-CAP

In this chapter:

- We've taken an overview of the teenage years, the different worlds which we and they are now living in; asking questions about ourselves as much as about our teenagers.
- We've looked at some of the changes that have arisen and are continuing to evolve, along with some of the strategies for negotiating these changes.
- We've looked not so much for problems and differences as growth points in understanding; to overcome barriers, build bridges and reduce spaces between us.

TAKING IT FURTHER

At the end of each chapter we want to give you a practical suggestion to take away and work on. We've included this in the book because we believe that there's real value in putting things into action straight away. We all have much more chance of effecting real change in our family's life, and in our relationships, if we don't just read about things but do them as well! So we would encourage you to 'take it further' and to take some practical steps before moving on to the next chapter.

Your first task in 'taking it further' is to do a review of the year for each of your teenagers.

REVIEW OF THE YEAR

The purpose of this review is to give you, as a parent, time and space to think about how the parenting of each of your teenagers is going. Most of our parenting is done off the cuff, so this is an opportunity to spend time reflecting on certain things.

To help you do this, work through this list of questions (taken from *Parentalk* by kind permission of Care for the Family) and use them to consider what you need to spend time on and how best you can build up your teenager. We'd actually recommend that you do this once a year for each of your children, maybe on their birthday or at the beginning of each year. It can be fascinating to see how they have changed and developed, and also for you to set goals for the future.

For each child ask yourself:

- How has the last year been for them and for my relationship with them?
- What have been some of the frustrations in my relationship with my teenager? How could we tackle them?
- What are some of the things we enjoy? How could we build in more opportunities for these things?
- Which of my teenager's strengths and abilities can I encourage?
- What do they really struggle with? How can I help?
- What is likely to be the next hurdle for them? How can I help?
- How are they getting on with the family and other friends?
- Having looked back and forward, what are the three 'must dos' for them in the next month or year?
- What do I think my child would wish for in the coming year?

Chapter 2
ON THE RADAR SCREEN
Teenage Communication

ON THE RIGHT WAVELENGTH

Everyone knows that communication is the key to relationships.

SYNCHRONISING WAVELENGTHS

But words don't always come easily to teenagers, as shown by some questions and answers collected from some GCSE exam papers. (These are all genuine responses.)

Q: Explain the processes by which water can be made safe to drink.
A: Flirtation makes water safe to drink because it removes large pollutants like grit, sand, dead sheep and canoeists.

Q: What guarantees may a mortgage company insist on?
A: If you are buying a house, they will insist you are well endowed.

Q: In a democratic society, how important are elections?
A: Very important. Sex can only happen when a male gets an election.

Q: What is the fibula?
A: A small lie.

Q: What is a terminal illness?
A: When you are sick at the airport.

Q: What is a seizure?
A: A Roman emperor.

Q: What are steroids?
A: Things for keeping carpets still on the stairs.

Parent to teenager: 'I'd like a word with you. Or two words out of you – whichever is easier!'

Communicating with our teenagers isn't always easy. We only need take a glance at this table to recognise the gulf between adults and teenagers:

The way adults tend to communicate	The way teenagers tend to communicate
By using reason, logic – prefer to stick to one topic at a time.	Stream of consciousness, easily switching between topics – like surfing the net or switching TV channels.
To solve problems, get results, change behaviour.	By talking at length without necessarily looking for solutions.
By lecturing or moralising, at times getting heavy and intense.	Like to leave things open-ended; don't need to have a point; enjoy talking for its own sake.
Interrogation-style! 'Have you. . .?' 'Are you. . .?' 'Aren't you. . .?'	Open up when least expect it and usually not to order.
Pushing to know the whole situation to learn from the details.	Less focused; more easily distracted; shorter attention span.
Generally in a hurry. Have high expectations of what can be achieved in a short amount of time.	Can't rush them. They are on their own timetable and often it's very slow.
Value listening – try not to interrupt.	Don't mind interrupting. If a thought is in their head, it's on their lips.

Adapted by Nicky and Sila Lee from Tim Smith, *Almost Cool*, Moody Press 1997.

Clearly communication between adults and teenagers is not easy. It can be frustrating because we're coming at a subject from different angles, with different objectives and with very different methods.

Stop & Think

In what ways does this chart describe some of the communication with your own teenagers?

Rob Parsons, with whom you may identify here, describes the moment he realised that things had changed for him and his son:

> When you turned thirteen it was as if you'd read somewhere about how teenagers are meant to behave and decided to do it all at once. On the eve of your birthday I said goodnight to a smiling, talkative 12-year-old. How was I to know that during the night, gremlins from the teenage farm were going to work you over? When you woke for school the next day you grunted at me. What I didn't know then was that this grunt was to be the highpoint of our communication for the next six years – from there it went downhill.

Bible View:

God can reassure and encourage us on any communication issues with our teenagers, and we in turn can reassure them. God's comfort communicates across every barrier.

'Praise be to the God and Father of our Lord Jesus Christ, the Father of compassion and the God of all comfort, who comforts us in all our troubles, so that we can comfort those in any trouble with the comfort we ourselves have received from God' (2 Corinthians 1:3–4).

PICKING UP THE SIGNALS

So how do we even begin to communicate with our teenagers if, first, they are so different from us and, secondly, they often don't want us to anyway?

A psychologist, Haim Ginott, says, 'Parents of teenagers face a difficult dilemma: how to help when help is resented, how to guide when guidance is rejected, how to communicate when attention is taken as attack.'

Here are some pointers:

SHOW AN INTEREST IN THEIR WORLD

Show an interest in their world, even if you don't understand everything. One of the most powerful ways to show your teenager that you care, and that you want to have meaningful communication, is to take an interest in what is happening to them and to learn the details of their lives. To find out those details, ask about them.

In other words, rather than asking, 'How was school today?' try asking, 'What did your art teacher say about your project on inner-city life?' It's easier and faster to ask, 'How was football today?' than to say, 'I'd love to hear about the match. Who else was on the team?'

But in taking an interest in the specific details of their lives – in their friends, their music, their favourite programmes, their 'heroes' – we prove to them that their world is important to us.

Stop & Think

What programmes, music, magazines, etc. influence your teenager? Do you know anything about them? Have you dismissed or criticised their choices in any way?

ADJUST TO THEIR TIMING

Teenagers have their own timing for everything – meals, bedtime, homework – and they choose the moments when they will disclose things to you and when they will let you in. We've found that many of the most meaningful conversations happen at the most inconvenient times. So we need to respond to the moment.

One incident that Paul will never forget was when our youngest daughter, Julia (who was about 17 at the time), was involved with a band, and they were playing at various pubs and clubs ('open-mic nights' to them) around London. Unfortunately, her instrument is the cello – not the easiest one to carry around!

This particular night she was playing at a club in north London, and it was when she told us that her 'set' didn't even start until midnight that we realised it was going to be a late one. Anyway, she reassured us that she would be making her own way back with friends.

We woke up at around 3 am and found that she still wasn't home, so we rang her mobile, only to find that she was waiting for a bus at Oxford Circus all by herself. Paul immediately said that he would go and pick her up, to which she tried to insist that she was fine – mainly because she was so worried that Paul would be furious with her.

On the way to collect her in the car, Paul decided to pull himself together and stay calm. So when he found her standing at the bus stop with only a few night-shift rubbish collectors for company, he was quite cheerful. Julia was so surprised and relieved that he was in such good humour that she talked animatedly all the way home. In fact, Paul took a detour because he said he was learning more about how she was doing in that car journey home than he had in the past six months!

Many conversations happen when we are doing very ordinary things with our children, when they feel relaxed and safe alongside us (not necessarily talking eyeball to eyeball). Standing around in the kitchen before or after meals is a popular place for casual conversation. It's a setting where they don't feel trapped or on the spot.

So often we found good conversations happened when we were tidying up after a meal, when we'd been looking for really good quality time over the meal. We'd tried to steer the conversation over supper to talk about meaningful things, but there'd been no response. But what we found time and again was that it all happened over the washing up. It was then that they would suddenly come out with things like 'Mum, what do you think about. . .?' or 'Dad, did you know. . .?'.

So what can we do to create the climate or atmosphere in which these encounters more readily take place? It's so important to learn to read the signs; to watch out for the casual 'Oh, by the way', which often means they've got to the point of the conversation when we thought it was all over. Or just when we're ready to turn the light off, they come and flop themselves on the end of our bed and want to have a heart to heart.

We remember a particular incident when we were all on the way to catch the channel ferry at four o'clock in the morning, having had about three hours' sleep the night before. We'd packed the car and got our three very disgruntled teenagers out of bed and into the back of the car at some unearthly hour – it had been a short night and it was going to be a very long day. We were halfway to Dover, and Paul was just beginning to relax after the stress of the departure. We thought the children were still all half-comatose, when a voice from the back seat suddenly piped up, 'Dad, what is homophobia?'

Stop & Think

When have you found you've had your best conversations with your teenagers? How were these conversations initiated?

LISTEN TO THEIR CONCERNS

The most important part of communication, and for many of us the most difficult, is learning to listen. Our teenagers need to know that we've heard them. Listening to them may be one of the most powerful ways of making a connection with them. Daniel Hahn says: 'The more a child becomes aware of a parent's willingness to listen, the more a parent will begin to hear.'

Good listening begins with reading the signs. The only way we

READING THE SIGNS

will find out what is going on inside another person is if we take time to look at them, to notice their struggles, to be sensitive to their insecurities. For example, a teenager's destructive behaviour or sullen mood often hides a cry for attention. We need to look beneath the surface.

This is one parent's experience:

> Lucy was so critical of everyone that I found it too hard to listen, so I broke all the rules and started telling her all that was wrong with her. She screamed back at me to shut up and then burst into tears. That was when I put my arms around her and did start to listen. It all poured out – she must have talked through her sobs for about an hour. Then her tears stopped and she said, 'Do you want a cup of tea?' Just like that – she was like a different person once she'd got her feelings out.

It's important to acknowledge some of the bad listening habits we all slip into. Here are some pointers on how to listen *badly*.

- Switch off whenever you think you know what your teenager is going to say.
- When you hear a phrase that makes you angry, like 'everyone else is going' or 'everyone else is allowed', explode and cut across them before they've finished.
- Make sure you always look distracted and glassy-eyed when your teenager is talking, then they can be sure you haven't really heard them.
- Always concentrate on the subject being talked about rather than the person speaking, then you're sure to miss all the non-verbal clues about how they feel.
- Make sure that you talk about important things when you're already in the middle of a stressful situation, such as rushing for a deadline or in a traffic jam, then you're sure to be able to respond to them irrationally.

I'm sure we all recognise something of ourselves in that list!

The fact is, we can all learn to be better listeners, and instead of constantly finding ourselves getting hooked into correcting our teenagers, or interrupting, or laying down the law, or even just consoling and trying to fix things, we can help them instead to talk about their thoughts and feelings.

Stop & Think

Think of one occasion recently when you've either listened well or listened badly. If it was a positive experience, what helped you to listen? If it was a negative experience, what hindered you from listening? Why do you think you were unable to hear or to pick up the signals?

RESPOND TO THEIR ISSUES

Real listening is the gateway to good responding. The most common things that stop us from reacting well to our teenagers are often our own anxieties, fears, anger and time pressures. All these things prevent us from responding openly, and, just as importantly, stop our teenagers from being open with us.

Here are some examples. Look at how the parents react in each of the following situations:

James: 'Why are you treating me like a child?'
Parent: 'Because you behave like a child.'

Clare: 'I don't care.'
Parent: 'No, you never think of anybody but yourself.'

Pete: 'My mates all say pot is harmless.'
Parent: 'Well, they're just stupid.'

Sarah: 'I've nobody to go to the disco with.'
Parent: 'Maybe it's just as well. You can save the money.'

In each of these situations the parents are failing to hear what is being said and to recognise what is going on under the surface.

Stop & Think

What do you think will be the result of interactions like these between parents and teenagers? Can you think of replies that would be more appropriate?

Bible View:

Some have said that God gave us two ears and only one mouth because it takes twice as much effort to listen as to speak. Certainly we all need the reminder to be quick to do the first and slow to do the second.

'Take note of this: Everyone should be quick to listen, slow to speak and slow to become angry' (James 1:19).

The first (listening) expresses sympathy, while the second (speaking) tends merely to express opinion.

TUNING IN TOGETHER

TUNING IN

We need to plan family time into our schedule so that we regularly connect with each other. Otherwise it's so easy to find that we might all be living in the same house but we're not really living with each other.

Time together as a family may be something that comes naturally to you – you're all used to sitting down and talking together, having meals as a family. For others, family life already seems to have dissipated into everyone doing their own thing, and family time would feel quite an awkward thing to initiate. But we would encourage you to see the family as an incredibly important base for your children through these teenage years.

What can the family offer our children through their teenage years? Here are four ingredients to think about:

SHARED IDENTITY

In so many other areas of their lives our teenagers are having to find themselves and prove themselves, so the family should provide a safe place. We mustn't belittle what the family can offer our teenagers.

If family identity is strong, and our teenagers feel involved in and proud to belong to their family, they are more likely to hold on to its values and principles. If they feel uninvolved and have little sense of belonging, they are more likely to look outside the family for a sense of identity.

SHARED VALUES

The family can play a crucial role in helping teenagers to think through their ideas and beliefs. We can help them work out what they believe is really important in life; what their core values are and how they can live by them. If they don't understand what they believe or why, our teenagers will be swept along with the latest craze or whim. We may find they have very little confidence to resist negative peer pressure and they will be tempted to do things simply to be liked by others.

What would you say are your family's top three values, and how have you communicated them and passed them on to your teenagers? For example, if one of your family values is compassion, your teenager may catch that value from you in the way you speak about people who are weak or ill or needy. They may see that value worked out by the way you look after an elderly person, regularly inviting them for lunch with the family; or by sponsoring a project together in a third world country or working together as a family one day on an inner-city project.

We have been involved in a prison and ex-offenders ministry in our church. This has included having a group of ex-offenders for Christmas lunch, which was great fun for us as a family.

Our children particularly remember it because we decided to cook fajitas, as the guys were cooking themselves a Christmas lunch the next day and didn't want turkey two days in a row. And as Christine was putting all the different fajita dishes on the table, to the children's horror she apparently said, 'This is a sort of smash and grab job!' They've never let her forget it.

We also had an opportunity to take Max into a prison with us when he'd just turned 19, and he spent a morning in the juvenile centre talking with some young lads. It was very special to share an experience like that together.

Or if one of your values is honesty, your teenager may catch that value from you in the way they see you talking to people, in how you handle money or in the way you recount events. They may see that value worked out by the way you expect them to be honest about where they've been, what they've been doing and who they've been with. They understand that within the family there is an expectation of trust and openness, not of secrets and half-truths.

Stop & Think

What do our teenagers pick up from us in the way they hear us talking to others over the phone, maybe pretending or offering one thing and saying quite another when we put the phone down?

Another of your values may be loyalty, and your teenager may catch that particular value from you in the way you stick up for people, maybe particularly those who are being maligned or ridiculed. They may see that value worked out by the way you appreciate long-term friendships and by the way you stand by each other within the family, even when things go wrong, and you believe in the best for each other.

Bible View:

So the values our teenagers pick up from us will be those they see we are committed to, concerned for, talk about and model in our own lives. Moses modelled the number one value in the Bible by saying:

'Love the Lord your God with all your heart and with all your soul and with all your strength. These commandments that I give you today are to be upon your hearts. Impress them on your children. Talk about them when you sit at home and when you walk along the road, when you lie down and when you get up' (Deuteronomy 6:5–7).

In passing on values remember: 'Values are something to do *with* our teenagers, not *to* our teenagers!'

Stop & Think

Having thought about your family's top three values, consider how your teenager would catch those values from you. How are you working this out in your family life?

SHARED EXPERIENCES

Carving out time when we can all be together, making plans, telling 'in' jokes, sharing stories, expressing anxieties, keeps the family close and protects individual members from becoming isolated or vulnerable.

We've found the best way to have family time is over a nice meal. We put great effort into making it feel special – candles, music, proper pudding! Although we remember that one of our first efforts at building in family time was quite revealing.

Don't you find that as soon as you make anything a priority, everything and anything will come against it? For us it was the phone. The phone must have rung half a dozen times during our quality family supper time, and finally Max jumped up from the table and said, 'I'll answer it.' Paul and I looked admiringly at each other over the table and said, 'Such a good boy – so kind and thoughtful. . .' Meanwhile, he picked up the phone and in a theatrical whisper simply said, 'Go away!'

We learned an important lesson that day.

When the children were younger it was much easier to plan family time. They all worked around our schedule, and we would nearly always do something together on a Friday night. It became much harder when they were older and they each had their own plans.

Many families we know find a regular time on a Sunday, when there are often fewer social distractions for the teenagers. They may have an early supper together or a late breakfast, but it's a time when the whole family gathers together.

Sometimes it might be helpful to have an 'agenda'; perhaps there is a holiday to plan, a gap year to discuss, work opportunities or other changes about to happen. It's often good to have something in mind to talk about, something that will involve you all, so that the time is focused and not wasted.

Don't be afraid to discuss controversial issues such as lifestyle, sex and drugs; or other big issues. Throw out a question such as, 'Why do you think people go hungry?' or 'Do you think city life is more likely to be violent?'

Share stories about yourself when you were their age – they love hearing about your misdemeanours at school, or your first boy or girlfriend, or your first job. Show them that you were a real teenager too!

SHARED FEELINGS

This is more than just understanding the nuts and bolts of family life; in other words, the arrangements, the timetables, who's in for what meal, etc. It's about getting to the feelings beneath the surface.

One of the most effective ways we found to encourage this sort of communication as a family was to use the little phrase: 'Mad, bad, sad, or glad?' Over a family meal we would go round the table and give everyone a chance to tell us something that had happened that week that had made them feel 'mad' (angry or cross), 'bad' (guilty or uneasy), 'sad' (upset or hurt) or 'glad' (good or happy). We often had teenage groans whenever we suggested it, but it nearly always uncovered something we would never otherwise have heard about. And one of the most important things that it always achieved was to encourage us all to talk about feelings, not just events.

Other families we know use the expression 'high/low' to each other – in other words, 'What have been your high points and low points of the day?' If used regularly it can be a very simple but meaningful little formula for connecting with each other at various points in the day; for example, over a cup of tea, as you say goodnight or when you're cooking supper.

We need to give our teenagers a chance to express their feelings about the day-to-day things that are happening to them. If we don't keep in touch with the small things we may well miss the significant moments. Encouraging them to talk at a deeper level, giving them an increased awareness of how they respond to people and situations, will be a wonderful gift to them as they head into the outside world.

TYPICAL TEENAGE SCENES

1. From being a chatty 12-year-old, my 14-year-old son is now completely monosyllabic. He seems moody and unhappy, and I'm worried that he's hiding something from me. How can I get him to communicate?

2. My two teenage daughters are constantly fighting – nearly always about clothes that they've borrowed from each other. They are both very different and don't seem to have anything in common, which just widens the gulf between them. How can I help them to get on with each other?

3. My daughter always has to have the last word and this causes real friction between us. What can I do?

FOLLOW-UP QUESTIONS

- How could you encourage your family to meet together regularly?
- Do your teenagers have a strong sense of family identity?
- Is there any particular person in your family who is more vulnerable or isolated at the moment?
- How have you encouraged your family to express their feelings and emotions?

RE-CAP

In this chapter:

- We've discussed the different issues involved in communicating with our teenagers.

- We've taken a look at our listening skills, learning to read between the lines of what is said on the surface of one-word sentences!
- We've looked at the importance of the whole family spending time together, communicating at the level of feelings.

TAKING IT FURTHER

- If you don't do it already, suggest having a regular family meal together once a week. Begin this week.
- Try out one of the suggestions on how to express your feelings ('mad, bad, sad or glad' or 'high/low').

Chapter 3
BUILT TO LAST
Teenage Character

THE FOUNDATION OF INNER STRENGTH

In Chapter 5 we will be looking at some of the biggest and most daunting issues facing our teenagers – the pressures of drugs, sex and alcohol. In this chapter we want to look at a number of things that will directly affect our teenagers' vulnerability to those pressures: their sense of worth, their strength of character and their basis for security.

All these things will affect how they respond when the pressure is on, and so it's really useful to consider these things and work on them before we start tackling the big issues.

BUILDING SELF-ESTEEM

This poem by Dorothy Low Nolte is entitled 'Children learn what they live':

If a child lives with criticism, he learns to condemn.
If a child lives with hostility, he learns to fight.
If a child lives with ridicule, he learns to be shy.
If a child lives with shame, he learns to feel guilty.
If a child lives with tolerance, he learns to be patient.
If a child lives with encouragement, he learns confidence.
If a child lives with praise, he learns to appreciate.

If a child lives with fairness, he learns justice.
If a child lives with security, he learns to have faith.
If a child lives with approval, he learns to like himself.
If a child lives with acceptance and friendship, he learns to find love in the world.

Stop & Think

Which of the following characteristics describe your teenager (even just a little)?

- witty
- relaxed
- likes to be asked for an opinion
- responsible with younger children
- idealistic
- energetic
- accepts people's differences
- loves fun
- supportive
- asks questions that force me to rethink my standards
- understands me
- keeps me young and in touch

It's good to remind ourselves of all the good qualities in our teenager. We need to let our teenager know about the good things we see in them. Our teenager needs constant reassurance that they're special.

Bible View:

Generous care, encouraging praise, supportive comfort and urging affirmation – these have always been the true qualities of parenthood, and they are needed more than ever in the teenage years.

> 'We were gentle among you, like a mother caring for her little children. . . we dealt with each of you as a father deals with his own children, encouraging, comforting and urging you to live lives worthy of God' (1 Thessalonians 2:7, 11–12).

So remind yourself of some of the good qualities in your teenager and consider how you could let them know about the good things you see in them.

Adolescence

The word 'adolescence' means 'the period of growth into maturity'. Three words contained within that definition give us an indication of what is ahead:

- *Period*: this is just a stage in their lives, so don't despair. It won't last for ever. And it's a good reminder for us as parents that this is a unique time, it will never happen again, so we need to make the most of it.
- *Growth*: it will involve change, so we need to be prepared.
- *Maturity*: there is a goal to aim for, so be encouraged to focus on the end result, not just all the minor details in between.

The teenage years mark a time of enormous change:

Physical changes

We would be hard pushed to include the complete list of physical changes taking place during the teenage years. Suffice it to say, the list is a long one. But as parents we need to be aware of two things concerning the changes: first, how fast these changes happen. Our son Max grew nearly six inches in one year! Secondly, how unpredictable the timetable of physical changes is – which can be agonising for late developers and excrutiatingly embarrassing for early developers.

Mental and emotional changes

It's a time when they're working out what they think about life and all it throws at them. This may mean that they challenge, even reject, your values and standards as they work things out for themselves. During these years they hit a roller-coaster of emotions. The highs are mountain-tops, the lows are deep troughs – very little is just normal.

Social changes

Their peer group becomes increasingly important. What this group says and how it acts and reacts to things will govern a large part of our teenager's behaviour. A teenager will do anything to get and keep acceptance among their peers, and this group may well begin to feel like a substitute family.

Sexual changes

Pre-puberty a boy will ignore or tease girls to keep them away. When he hits puberty he will ignore or tease girls to make them notice him. Girls used to annoy him – now they attract him. They're like a magnet!

All these changes can cause great insecurity and confusion. During these adolescent years our teenagers constantly question themselves:

- What am I really like?
- How do I come across to others?
- What do other boys/girls think of me?
- Am I really as ugly as I think I am?

Their answers to these questions will be mostly negative unless they have developed a healthy self-esteem.

Helping our teenagers to think of themselves in a right and positive way will be one of the greatest gifts we can give them as they face the outside world.

Good self-esteem is the secret ingredient that helps get many young people through adolescence relatively unscathed. It's probably one of the strongest weapons we can give our teenagers to cope with pressure from peers, enabling them to resist doing or achieving things simply to be liked by others.

Paul remembers telling Max how much he admired his natural confidence with people, and admitted how he himself always felt so under-confident as a teenager. This surprised and encouraged Max, as all he had ever known was a father who spoke and related to others so easily.

Others will judge our teenagers on what they do or what they look like. We, as parents, must show them that we love and accept them, not for what they can achieve, but for who they are – with no strings attached.

If your teenager isn't sure that you love them in this sort of way, they'll most likely go looking for love elsewhere, and very often they'll end up looking in all the wrong places. For example, teenagers who feel unsure of their parents' love are more likely to be sexually promiscuous, or may be more vulnerable to illnesses such as anorexia and bulimia.

Unconditional love means loving our children no matter what we expect them to be and, most difficult, no matter how they behave.

Stop & Think

When do we find it most difficult to love our teenager? What matters most to us? Is it what they look like, good exam results, good manners, sporting achievements, job prospects, not smoking, not taking drugs, keeping a faith? Or something else?

Young children grow up instinctively loving and trusting their parents, and they take it for granted that we love them. Teenagers question all their previous assumptions, including our love and acceptance of them. So we need to work extra hard through these years to give them absolute proof that we still love them; that we'll always love them, no matter what happens.

How do we encourage a healthy self-esteem in our teenagers? What are the signs to look out for to suggest whether they have good or low self-esteem?

A teenager with good self-esteem will tend to:

- take on new experiences willingly;
- be open to making new friends;
- be happy not always to be the centre of attention;
- be generous with praise of other people's achievements;
- treat others with consideration;
- not be too judgemental of others;

- be prepared to admit their own mistakes;
- be able to take positive criticism.

A teenager with low self-esteem will tend to:

- shy away from new experiences;
- be very protective of existing friends and suspicious of new ones;
- be in more constant need of reassurance;
- be too competitive in areas where they feel confident;
- blame others for their mistakes;
- find assurance in the faults of others;
- get angry and defensive when criticised;
- feel they have to constantly do things to make others like them, e.g. give presents, lend things, clown around or do favours.

One parent, after reading these lists, rather candidly said, 'That describes me as well as my teenager!'

Stop & Think

Which of these different characteristics can you already see developing in your teenager? Which need special encouragement? Your teenager is probably a mixture of these two lists, but which one best describes them?

Teenagers, like adults, feel good about themselves when they know they're doing well. And they know they're doing well when they're *told* they're doing well. Our teenagers need to feel valued and appreciated, and they will only feel these things when they hear us giving specific and positive input. We can so easily get into negative patterns with them and we need to watch ourselves. We were brought up short by one of ours not long ago when they commented: 'Why is it you always notice when I do something wrong, but never when I do something right?'

A healthy habit to get into is to aim to tell our teenager each day at least one positive thing they've done and this will reverse any negative spiral. A good motto for parents of teenage children would be: 'Catch your teenager doing something right, and praise them for it.'

It's particularly important for fathers to praise their teenagers. Their approval is so important through these years: for girls to hear their father saying that they're beautiful and precious; for boys to hear their father admiring and affirming them.

So whether it's spoken directly to them or written down in a card or a letter (so they can read it to themselves again and again), praise will help your teenager's self-esteem to blossom.

We were really touched when we visited Julia while she was doing one of her university terms in Italy. We had sent her a card telling her how proud we were of how she was managing on her own, and how excited we were with all she was doing. We noticed when we looked around the room where she was staying that she'd stuck the card up beside her bed with a number of others. But the interesting thing was that she'd put it up with the message showing rather than the pretty picture, because she said she wanted to be able to read it whenever she glanced up.

How can we most effectively praise our teenagers?

Here are a few pointers as to what praise should be.

Specific rather than general

Always be specific. If your teenager knows exactly what they did right, they'll learn to recognise their strengths. Don't just say, 'That was good.' Explain why it was good.

Genuine rather than patronising

Never let your desire to praise your child push you into lying to them. Insincere praise never works. Not only is it patronising, but it will devalue any genuine praise you give on future occasions.

Paul, at one stage, rather over-used the phrase 'I'm so proud of you' with our family, to the extent that our teenagers shortened it and would sign off their notes and birthday cards to him rather sarcastically with *S.P.O.Y.*!

About effort rather than achievement

If your teenager begins to link your approval and love with their success, the self-esteem you're trying to build will be destroyed. So make sure you praise them just as much for their efforts, choices, thoughtfulness, ideas or helpfulness as for success itself.

We set up a tradition in our family that each child would choose to go somewhere special for a few days with Mum or Dad as a treat for doing their exams. So *before* the results came out we would celebrate all the effort they'd put in.

Straightforward rather than comparing

Never ask, 'Were you better than so and so?' And don't praise your teenager for *being* the best. *Doing* their best is what counts. Help them to measure their effort against their own standards, not someone else's.

We've found that this is a really important one to watch out for when we read their reports or exam results. Our three have had very different gifts and abilities, and we've realised that it's been crucial to encourage them individually and make sure they don't feel we're comparing them with each other or that they're competing against each other.

Unconditional, with no strings attached

Never praise them simply to warm them up for a favour; for example, 'That's really great, love. . .now could you get us a cup of tea?' Even if your praise is real, by linking it to a request you'll make it sound insincere.

About gifts rather than bribes

Don't give incentives like, 'If you do well in your exams I'll get you that ipod you want.' If they fail, you'll find yourself having to withhold a present just when your teenager needs to feel your love and acceptance the most. Try not to use treats as incentives.

Unqualified rather than half-hearted

If you follow your praise with a lecture on how they could have done even better if only they'd done this or that, you'll send your teenager the message that their effort wasn't good enough.

Stop & Think

Which of these forms of praise are you prone to getting wrong? In what ways and on what occasions have you most effectively praised your teenager?

THE BUILDING MATERIALS

FILLING THE EMOTIONAL TANK

Do you know the most important question on your teenager's mind? Your teenager may never verbalise it or even consciously acknowledge it, but he or she is continually asking: 'Do you love me?' – usually by what they do rather than what they say.

Ross Campbell says, 'A teenager is the most vulnerable person in society, and his deepest need is love.' We often miss it because we see them as these fast-growing, independent, often quite prickly beings who don't want us to get too close. But we must remember through these years that *we* are still their main source of love and affirmation, even though it may not feel like it much of the time.

We're all aware that there are an unprecedented number of outside influences upon our teenagers, many of them unwholesome, and some are actually bad influences and potentially very harmful. A teenager who doesn't feel loved and cared for is highly vulnerable to those influences.

In this section we're going to look at how we as parents can help to meet our teenagers' emotional needs. So much of their time is spent under the control and influence of others, we can begin to wonder what our role is (apart from cook, chauffeur and general nagger). But at this stage of their lives it's vital not to underestimate the influence of the home.

Parents should still be the ones to top up their teenagers' emotional tanks. The tank is figurative, of course, but the concept is very real. We all know that a car only runs with petrol or diesel in its fuel tank. What fuel does a human being (a teenage human being) need?

Well, they all need food. If we've got teenage boys in the house we're probably very aware that food consumption has shot up. If we have teenage girls we're probably aware of other problems with food (faddish diets or unhealthy eating habits).

They all need money too; for mobile phones, travel, clothes, going out – the list can feel endless!

But there is another tank that needs filling up even more than these, and that is the tank of their emotional resources. At this stage in their lives their bodies are playing havoc with their emotions – their hormones are all over the place. How do we as parents react to their roller-coaster of emotions? Are we always negative – rather like kicking the car because it's run out of petrol when of course what we need to do is put more petrol in it? In fact we should have had our eye on the petrol gauge and seen it coming. We should have seen the warning light flashing instead of waiting until it was too late.

So what exactly do we mean by 'topping up the emotional tank'? We mean fulfilling their emotional needs. We all have certain emotional needs, and whether these emotional needs are met (through love, understanding, discipline and so on) helps determine how we feel (whether we are content, angry, depressed or happy). Also it strongly affects our behaviour (whether we're confident or difficult people, playful or withdrawn).

The fuller the tank is, the more positive the feelings and the better the behaviour. Only when their emotional tank is full can a teenager be expected to *be* their best and *do* their best. But how in practice, in everyday life, can we make sure that we are filling up our teenager's emotional tank? One very helpful tool is to discover the primary ways they feel loved. They have been described as the love languages.

THE LOVE LANGUAGES

Bible View:

Discovering the appropriate expression of love for each individual is the most caring thing we can do for them.

'The only thing that counts is faith expressing itself through love' (Galatians 5:6).

It's all about looking at the different ways in which we can express love to them. And in practice there are five ways through which we can actively show love:

1. Words: of appreciation, encouragement, kindness; words that make requests not demands.
2. Time: being available when they need to talk.
3. Affection: hugs, jokes, comfort.
4. Presents: little things that show you have been thinking of them (not necessarily the latest gadget).
5. Actions: giving them a lift when it's raining, cooking their favourite meal.

These are all practical ways in which we can communicate love. These ways of putting love into action are called 'the five love languages' in a book of the same name by Gary Chapman, in which he uses the metaphor of language to examine the different ways in which we communicate and understand love.

He points out that we all have a 'native language' that we find most natural to speak and comprehend, and then many people have a second language or more. So too each of us has a first 'love language' through which we most easily understand love, though we'll appreciate it in other ways as well.

Every expression of love can be put under one of these headings: words, time, affection, presents or actions. For example:

- Giving them cash to buy a ticket for their night out = presents.
- Picking them up from school when it's raining = actions.
- Stopping to watch a programme on TV with them = time.
- Giving them a hug as they go out of the door = affection.
- Telling them they've done a good job on the washing up = words.

Now all of those five ways of showing love are important as we relate to our teenagers. But as we look at that list, we may already be aware of particular ways in which we're failing them – we're not caring for them and supporting them as we should. If that is the case we need to be aware of one or two habits that are easy to fall into.

Parents may become over-indulgent in a mistaken attempt to compensate. They may indulge with obvious materialistic things, such as clothes, gadgets, sports equipment; or with less obvious ones, such as allowing their teenagers to go to places they really shouldn't, or watch things that are unsuitable, or do things they're not really happy about, or stay out later than they know is wise. These things are often ways of compensating for a lack of emotional input and support.

The point of trying to discover our teenager's love language is not so much what we think they need from us, but what they feel they need from us. How best will they receive love from us and in what ways will they *feel* most loved by us? Our unthinking tendency is to give love in the way that we like to receive it, the way we understand it, and then we are left wondering why they are not responding or appreciating all our efforts. We need to understand their particular love language – how will they best feel that we love them?

Now each of us needs *all* of these five to make us feel loved, but one or perhaps two of these will be particularly important to our teenager at this point in time.

Stop & Think

Which of these love languages make your teenager feel most loved? Which is their 'native' language? Which others are particularly important?

A SECURE STRUCTURE

KEEPING GOD AT THE CENTRE

Bible View:

The teenage years are ones of growth in every way: physically, mentally, socially – and there is no reason why they should not also be tremendous times of growth in character and spiritual maturity, towards stability and independence.

'Then we will no longer be infants, tossed back and forth by the waves, and blown here and there by every wind of teaching and by the cunning and craftiness of men in their deceitful scheming. Instead, speaking the truth in love, we will in all things grow up into him who is the Head, that is, Christ' (Ephesians 4:14–15).

How can we help our teenagers to continue to grow in their Christian faith? What role can we expect to play in these teenage years when they need to discover things for themselves? We must realise that by their mid-teens it is too late for us to have any direct influence – they will be making their own choices. However, we can share the responsibility with others – for example, our church youth leaders, teachers, mentors and their peer group.

How can we as parents keep alongside them, encouraging but not 'swamping' them? Here are a few suggestions:

- We have to learn to let go – in this area of their lives as in any other. This will show itself in our reactions to the choices they make. They may not want to go to church, or they may want to explore a new one or even a different spiritual tradition. Are we prepared to let them go?

For a time Max decided to go to another church, and it was important that we affirmed that. This is part of a natural inclination to explore up to the limits and over the limits of your experience. We mustn't allow this to cause us to feel inadequate or defensive.

- Pray for them. These are the years when our prayers for them need to double. When our teenagers are outside of our reach/control, we realise in a new way that they are still within God's reach. We need to increase our efforts in prayer for our children through these teenage years.

Christine remembers vividly one particular night when Emily was at a party. She was due to be staying the night with a friend, so wasn't expected home, but Christine woke up with a start at 1.50 am, and felt a sudden urgency to pray for her. She asked, 'Lord, what should I pray?' The word came very simply, 'Turn the light on!' and she knew it was for Emily not for herself. So that's what she prayed over and over for about ten minutes, and then went back to sleep.

A few days later they were having a cup of coffee together, and Christine plucked up the courage to ask her whether there was anything significant in that prayer. Apparently, around that time at the party, Emily was on her own with a boy in the kitchen and she was just beginning to feel out of her depth when someone came in and turned the light on.

We are certain, in our own minds, that the timing was exact; that God woke us up to pray on her behalf. And we have heard many other stories, from other parents, who have been called to pray at particular times for their teenagers, and only later did it make sense.

(Emily admitted a few years later that this incident did make her think twice about doing anything naughty for a while – as 'God might tell Mum'!)

We realise in a fresh and vital way through these years that God is there when we are not.

- We mustn't belittle the indirect influence we can still have on them, both through our prayers and through other less obvious ways.

We have always encouraged our teenagers to go on Christian camps and house parties – both with us and, more importantly, without us. We always make sure that our own family holidays don't conflict with them, and that we have talked it through with them at an early stage of their planning, so that when other invitations come along these camps are already firmly on their agenda, not an after-thought that sadly doesn't quite happen.

We've also kept deliberate contact with other families with Christian teenagers. So, for example, we have spent various holidays with a couple of other church families, and it's proved a lovely way of maintaining contact between the teenagers.

- We would encourage parents to be very careful about any relocation during their children's teenage years. Now obviously there is not always a lot of choice in the matter, but if there is flexibility over timing, we would encourage parents to be careful about uprooting teenagers if they are in a stable and healthy Christian environment through these years.
- Put good Christian material around the house to motivate your teenagers to read and discuss different issues.

We've found that the chaps in our household love reading on the loo. They will avidly read anything left in the bathroom, so it's a perfect place to leave the latest good biography. Just make sure you've used the facilities before they get in there!

- Look out for good gap-year experiences. This is a terrific time to capture their imagination with a specific project and to link them up with other Christians of their own age and stage. These can often be life-changing experiences. Let's make sure God is at the centre of them.
- Always remain open for conversation. Let them know that you will always be there for them, whether they have rejected your values and beliefs or whether they have remained with them.

TYPICAL TEENAGE SCENES

1. My 15-year-old daughter really seems to dislike her appearance. She's always making comments about how big her nose is or how fat her thighs are. Nothing I say seems to make any impact. How can I help her?

2. My 14-year-old son has always been mediocre at sport, but he's desperate to be accepted by the sporty crowd in his year. I can see that they don't really include him, but he's now given up on his old friends to try to be part of this new group. I don't want him to be left with no friends at all. What should I do?

3. My 16-year-old son is struggling with the exam workload. He won't take advice and seems to have almost given up. My husband, who used to be a teacher, has tried to help him, but it always ends in raised voices and slammed doors. What should we do?

FOLLOW-UP QUESTIONS

- Do you relate personally to the suggestion that certain acts make you feel more loved than others?

- Do you agree on what your teenager's primary love languages are?
- How are you planning to feed these?

RE-CAP

In this chapter:

- We've looked at how our teenagers think about themselves.
- We've thought about how they feel secure and loved by us.
- We've asked how we can encourage them in their faith.

TAKING IT FURTHER

- Try out your teenager's top love language on them this week. See what impact it has.
- Try praising your teenager for something, however small, every day this week. See what impact it has.

Chapter 4
BOUNDARIES AND BATTLEFIELDS
Teenage Tensions

TO BOLDLY GO

EXPLORING THE LIMITS

In this chapter we're going to think through some of the battles that arise during these years.

Here are some 'house rules' you might like to adopt:

If you sleep on it. . .make it.
If you wear it. . .hang it up.
If you drop it. . .pick it up.
If you step on it. . .wipe it off.
If you open it. . .close it.
If you empty it. . .fill it.
If it rings. . .answer it.
If it howls. . .feed it.
If it cries. . .love it.

Like us, you might find it helpful to stick these on your fridge door for a while!

Set boundaries

Where do we set the boundaries? Seen on a teenager's badge were the words: 'I'm bored – forbid me to do something!'

Bible View:

The Bible has plenty of advice to parents and children in this regard. On the one hand:

'Children, obey your parents in the Lord. . . Honour your father and mother' (Ephesians 6:1).

On the other hand:

'Fathers, do not exasperate your children; instead, bring them up in the training and instruction of the Lord' (Ephesians 6:4).

Growing up involves moving from 'obey your parents' (for young children) to 'honour your father and mother' (for children of all ages). But this assumes the right to be obeyed and honoured. Parents who provoke their children with arbitrary demands are the opposite of those who nurture them by good example.

Through the teenage years we as parents should be moving from a place of parental control to one of parental trust – from controller to consultant. Daniel Hahn says:

> As hard as it is, our role must move from controller to consultant. What do consultants do? They ask questions, offer opinions, share experiences, present opinions and forecast outcomes. Ultimately, however, they step back and allow the client to make decisions. Consultants understand what they can and cannot do for their clients, and as a result the client owns the process as well as the results.

Our aim is to move from giving them externally imposed boundaries to helping them develop internal self-imposed boundaries. At this stage one of the most important principles to make them understand is that *privileges and freedom depend on trustworthiness.*

A wise move, therefore, for us as parents is to start off with fairly fixed boundaries, so that as time goes on we are able to allow more privileges rather than fewer. The point is this: if you begin by being careful and restrictive you can then afford to be positive and generous. But if you begin by being broad-minded, reasonable and understanding (for example, offering too many privileges/too few restrictions) you've only one way to go, which is increased restrictions.

Encourage responsibility

Set up firm expectations at the beginning that allow you to be as positive as possible. We need to retain the option to reward our teenagers where they've been responsible. If curfew time is always late or vague, we haven't left ourselves room to be generous. Whereas if the norm is ten o'clock on school nights and they respect that, we can afford to offer an extension on a special occasion.

On their part, we're looking for consideration – keeping us informed of where they are and who they're with. And on our part, there should be a willingness to listen to their requests. These two things working together allow for flexibility and understanding between us.

So, for example, if they are wanting to stay out late on a particular night we negotiate with them. It's not a straight 'yes' or 'no'. Instead we ask questions like: Are they with friends we trust? Are they going to be at a place we feel secure about? Have they caught up on sleep recently? Are they doing something legitimate that warrants extra time? Do they have early commitments in the morning? This all helps us and them to build up a clear picture.

We need to work out boundaries with them that are fair – not just in our eyes, but in theirs too – ones that give them some degree of responsibility. As they get older, one of the most important things we can do as parents is to help them make choices that they can 'own', so that they learn to take responsibility for their own actions.

For example, how many of us still take responsibility for making sure our teenager gets up on time for school in the morning? How many of us start the day by calling up the stairs at least five times to wake them up, calling another five times to get them downstairs for breakfast, and nagging them yet again to get them out of the door to catch the bus?

We've got to realise that what we're doing is actually counter-productive. Our teenagers know that when we call up the stairs the first time there's absolutely no need to respond because they're going to get another call in five minutes' time, and another five minutes after that! What we're doing is actually encouraging irresponsibility. Isn't it time they took responsibility for getting to school on time, and bearing the consequences if they don't?

We remember making a very deliberate decision when our youngest started sixth form. He had been particularly laid back about mornings, so we sat him down and said to him, 'We're going to start doing things differently. From now on we're not going to be waking you up for school. It's going to be your responsibility to get yourself up in the morning and get out of the door on time.'

It was all done in good humour and with no ill feeling – in fact he quite liked the idea of not being nagged by the 'rentals' (parents) first thing in the morning!

All went well until one morning he didn't wake up until 11 am – and we didn't wake him. He got to school halfway through the morning and received the statutory ticking off. It never happened again.

We must stop pampering our teenagers. We don't help them by constantly covering for them. We've got to allow them to own their actions.

Christine looks back on the countless times she would do yet another run into school after a mid-morning phone call pleading for the forgotten football kit or musical instrument or packed lunch. She wonders now if a slightly firmer response might have initiated a raised level of responsibility and avoided all that unnecessary hassle.

If we are constantly bailing them out, they never face up to the consequences of their mistakes.

What are you doing for your teenagers that they could and should do for themselves? We've got to remember that one of our goals should be to prepare our teenagers for when they leave home and have to fend for themselves. Our aim should be to help them grow in confidence and responsibility so that this is an easy step for them – not a traumatic one.

Stop & Think

Which of the following tasks have we handed over or could we hand over to our teenagers?

- Preparing meals.
- Washing/ironing clothes.
- Helping with a younger sibling.
- Getting themselves up.
- Locking doors at night.
- Cleaning the bathroom.
- Settling their own arguments.
- Making decisions about their routine.

Parents who pamper have good intentions, but they can easily develop irresponsibility and even disrespect in their children without realising it. Rather than helping them grow up, we're keeping them young.

One of the things that used to cause most friction with our oldest daughter, Emily, was keeping to an agreed time to come in at night. Timing has never been her strongest point and it nearly always used to end up with her coming in late, us being kept awake, getting more and more anxious, and then blasting her off when she came in – mainly through worry and exhaustion.

One of the best tips we were given was to set an alarm clock outside our bedroom door for the time they were due in, and agree that it was their responsibility to turn it off before it went off. That meant two things: first, we could go to sleep, safe in the knowledge that we would be woken if they didn't come in. And secondly, it gave them a strong incentive to get back on time. But more importantly, it promoted the principle that is so important through these teenage years: that *privileges and freedom depend on trustworthiness.*

Be ready to say 'no'

We need a united front at these times. We need to be prepared to say 'no' to the teenage naggers who just wear us down. Teenagers are the most persistent creatures when they want something.

We also need to be prepared to say 'no' to the teenager who pushes for an immediate answer to a request made at the last minute.

We remember the many times we've had one of our teenagers on their mobile, saying something like, 'I'm going to a party and staying overnight with Elly. Is that OK? Mum, I'm running out of battery – I need to know *now*!'

And we must be prepared to say 'no' to the teenager who insists that everyone else's parents say it's OK. Our teenagers were often going to parties at homes where we didn't know the parents very well, if at all. The arrangements were often very 'loose' – an invitation from a friend whose boyfriend's friend knew the friend! And we would quite frequently insist on ringing the parents beforehand to check that it was all OK. We always had the same old battle with them over it, because they always insisted that we were the only parents 'on the planet' who ever did this.

Work out consequences

There must be consequences if they overstep the mark. These consequences must be something that makes an impact, something that 'bites'. They mustn't be too lenient or they will have no impact at all; but at the same time they mustn't be too harsh so that we drive our teenager into a corner. Most importantly for us as parents, they mustn't be too difficult for us to enforce. For example, there's no point telling a six-foot-tall teenage boy to go to his room if he's likely to stand his ground – you'll never move him! Max has been known to put Christine over his shoulder in a fireman's lift and dump her in the hallway when she threatened to turn off his TV programme!

The consequences we've found to be generally most effective are:

- reducing their TV time (Paul has even resorted to cutting the plug off the lead);
- stopping their allowance for a period of time;
- confiscating their mobile phone for a certain length of time (that one really hurts!);
- not allowing them to go to the next party, or 'grounding' them for the next weekend.

If used rightly, consequences can be very powerful – not just in showing our teenagers what they've done wrong, but in giving them an incentive to put things right. We heard of a family that initiated a 'Saturday Box'. The mother had got so frustrated with constantly clearing up all the debris that her teenagers left around the house, she made what she called a 'Saturday Box'. Into this box she would put anything her teenagers 'discarded' around the house during the week, apart from essentials such as homework or travel cards. Whenever they asked for these items during the week, she would say that they were quite safe and could be collected on Saturday from the box. Just one comment: this whole plan does, of course, require a little ingenuity in finding a place to hide the box from desperate teenagers.

What do we do when they cross over the boundary? There are many reasons why teenagers may have found themselves in trouble, and before we pass judgement we first need to ask ourselves why they crossed the boundary.

Did they cross the boundary without realising it? Did we make our expectations clear? If not, we need to spell them out.

Did they cross the boundary through error – was it just a mistake on their part? If this is the case, they need to be helped to avoid it next time.

Did they cross the boundary through immaturity or inexperience? Something may go wrong purely and simply because they are in a totally new situation. So our task is to help them learn the consequences of their actions.

Did they cross the boundary to get attention? Are they saying, 'The only way I'll get you to notice me is if I do something drastic'? This needs a deeper conversation after some soul-searching on our part.

Or did they cross the boundary to challenge us? We put this last, because this is sometimes our first conclusion. Is this a deliberate act of defiance of pushing the boundaries to see how far they can go? If so, this is one battle we must fight to win. If we're not firm now, they won't take us seriously again.

All these crossings need different handling, so you first need to be sure which one you're dealing with.

Stop & Think

Can you think of one incident that happened recently when your teenager crossed a boundary? Which of the five boundary crossings was made?

- Without realising?
- By an error?
- Through immaturity?
- For attention-seeking?
- In defiance?

Do you think you assessed the situation correctly at the time, or do you see it rather differently now?

A lot of this 'working out of boundaries' needs to be done between us as parents ahead of time, but if we're caught unawares (which we all will be occasionally) we need to have a clear policy of backing one another in front of them – even though we may disagree in private. Some of our most difficult times have been not so much a controversy with our teenagers over an issue, as a controversy between us as parents over how to handle it. This has often created far more friction and confusion in the family than the issue itself.

Teenagers very quickly sense when we are uncertain, and are very quick to exploit the situation and play one parent off against the other. Their policy tends to be 'divide and conquer' and they can become very skilful at it.

EMPIRE WARS

CHOOSING YOUR BATTLES

Throughout the teenage years we are working with a difficult balance of giving them increased independence and freedom, but still maintaining the boundaries for their own protection and development.

So choose your battles – don't pick a fight! If we fight every battle, our teenagers will never discover the ones that really do matter to us. So often we can fight battles that aren't worth the fight and we can end up worse enemies than before.

There are bound to be times when we fall out with our children, but we need to know when to fight and when to stand back – especially during the teenage years when there are so many more issues to work through.

When drawing up the battle plans consider these things first:

Always ask yourself: 'Is it worth the fight?'

Bible View:

The battles worth fighting are the ones that may bring lifelong benefit or avert lifelong harm, which is why the Bible tells us to:

'Train a child in the way he should go, and when he is old he will not turn from it' (Proverbs 22:6).

Stop & Think

What makes you angry? Which aspects of your teenager's behaviour make you angry again and again?

Generally, the things that annoy parents of teenagers the most are:

- staying up (or staying out) late at night;
- not getting up in the morning;
- moaning about or ignoring requests for help;
- spending hours on their mobiles/the internet/TV;
- not doing homework;
- loud music;
- being rude to parents or unkind to siblings.

Does all this sound familiar? Be assured that you are not alone – this is teenage life.

Christine remembers getting upset with Max because he refused to get a haircut for months on end, and it became quite an issue between them – especially when she discovered dreadlocks appearing (Paul said that he rather liked them, which didn't really help!). When Emily came home from university to find them still arguing about it, she simply said, 'Mum, just leave it – it's his choice now, not yours.' That brought Christine up short and made her realise it was her turn to back down.

It is the everyday things that can so easily annoy us. We need to ask ourselves, 'Is it really worth so much emotion?' If we think it does really matter, then we should ask ourselves: 'How can I change the situation or defuse the anger? How can I make things more bearable for both sides?'

Check yourself before you check them

Bible View:

Jesus said in the Sermon on the Mount:

'First take the plank out of your own eye, and then you will see clearly to remove the speck from your brother's eye' (Matthew 7:5).

The most common problems to affect our ability as parents to control our anger are feeling low, tiredness and worry.

Stop & Think

Are you aware of the effect these conditions have on you? Are you or have you been susceptible to any of these in particular? How does your teenager perceive this condition?

When we're under pressure, where possible we need to ask ourselves a number of searching questions. What is my emotional temperature? Am I worried about other things – for example work, money or health? Am I so upset about things generally that I'm just picking holes in nothing in particular – in other words, simply taking it out on them? And finally (one of the most useful), would it be better to 'cool off' first?

So we should check ourselves before we check them!

Learn how to face conflict; it isn't always a bad thing

> Bible View:
>
> In the book of Proverbs it says:
>
> 'Better is open rebuke than hidden love' (Proverbs 27:5).
>
> We are often tempted to avoid confrontation in the name of a misjudged love. But that can lead to denial, pretending we haven't seen something that needs to be dealt with, or double standards, reacting inconsistently.

Anger is normal and occurs in every human being. The problem is learning to manage it. Handling anger is one of the most difficult lessons in life – one that many adults never learn. Self-control is something we most need when we least want it. How do we keep control of ourselves? How do we ensure that we don't lose it when pushed?

There are three basic rules we need to try and follow. Three 'don'ts' to watch:

1. Don't over-react. Emotional over-reaction from us as parents is very destructive to the relationship if it happens too often and is not resolved.

2. Don't jump to conclusions, making sweeping generalisations. Our teenagers would often complain that Christine too readily assumed that parties are 'bad places where bad things happen'.

3. Don't be hurtful, attacking them rather than the problem; for example, using phrases such as 'You're so selfish', 'You're hopeless', 'You're totally unreliable'. How easily these little phrases trip off our tongue! We need to be particularly careful about using labels like these because teenagers often believe the names they are given and act accordingly.

When we're annoyed or upset, an 'I' message is a more effective and respectful way to treat our teenager than attacking them with a 'you' message. So instead of 'You're late again', we could say, 'I feel anxious when you don't come in at the agreed time.' Or instead of 'You always leave your clothes all over the floor', we could say, 'I feel used when you expect me to clear up after you.' And instead of 'You never show appreciation', we could say, 'I feel hurt when you never thank me.'

Expressing things in this way means that instead of putting the problem 'out there' between us and our teenager, we're instead being more open and honest about how *we* are feeling and how *we* are affected by their behaviour.

Stop & Think

Think of an incident recently when you attacked your teenager's character rather than the issue. How could you have spoken more helpfully?

Calm down. Shouting is just louder, not necessarily more effective!

Bible View:

The Bible compares the tongue to a fire (James 3:6). Fires can get out of control, and then they do damage. So too can a habit of reacting with louder and louder shouts or threats.

We all know that shouting is an ineffective form of discipline, but most of us continue to do it. Shouting generally tends to do little more than raise our blood pressure and stir our children up pretty effectively.

But when is it OK to shout? Well, there are different kinds of shouting:

- There's the 'Stop!' type of shouting, when your tone implies instant obedience for their safety (usually required for slightly younger children).
- There's the 'Oi, come here!' kind of shouting – useful for large gardens, loft extensions and teenagers with headphones plugged in.

Then there are the more unpleasant varieties:

- There's the sudden 'Let's get some action around here!' shouting, which demands instant obedience but denies any prior explanation or warning.
- There's the 'Oh, please come on' wearied whine type of shouting (otherwise known as nagging), or 'I'm not telling you again' (when that is what you are doing endlessly).

- There's the 'What the heck/past caring' style of shouting, when you've been shouting all day so you may as well shout some more!
- Then there's the full-blown 'I don't deserve this kind of treatment' adult version of a tantrum.

Do you recognise yourself in any of these?

Remember how important it is to say sorry and move on

Bible View:

In the New Testament we read:

'Fathers, do not embitter your children, or they will become discouraged' (Colossians 3:21).

Saying sorry and forgiving must work in both directions in all human relationships. In parent-teenager relationships it is the key to stemming a growing tide of resentments.

An apology may be one of the least costly and most rewarding investments we can make. We all get things wrong or over-react at times, and if we don't do it too often, it is possible to produce a positive situation out of a negative one. When we can apologise and admit getting it wrong, it can often strengthen and 'sweeten' a relationship that's gone sour.

A sincere apology may be the best way to take the heat out of a situation and change the atmosphere. For example: 'I know I got too angry and said things I didn't mean – I'm so sorry.' There is tremendous power in just saying a simple sorry and stopping there – no 'buts' or excuses or half-hidden lectures tacked on.

Stop & Think

When was the last time you apologised, or should have apologised, to your teenager?

AN ARMY OF CLONES

COPING WITH PEER PRESSURE

We cannot over-estimate the power of the peer group. It is probably one of the greatest and most powerful influences on our children. The pressure begins as soon as they start school and builds up to a peak through the teenage years.

At the heart of each of us is a need to belong, to be part of a group. And unless you conform to that group – in the way you dress, in the way you behave, in your likes and dislikes – you can feel that you don't belong, and that can be devastating. It's hard enough for an adult, so imagine the power it has on young people!

Bible View:

The desire to belong to a social group is part of the way we are wired:

> 'In Christ we who are many form one body, and each member belongs to all the others' (Romans 12:5).
>
> That instinct for community can be fulfilled in many ways, but the deepest and most satisfying way will feed our spiritual as well as our social dimension.

As young people move into the adolescent years, their emotions can run wild. In that emotional minefield, the desire to belong to a group is huge. When our children are young we have some influence over choosing their close peer group. When they move on to secondary school, most of that influence is taken away from us. Our teenagers will increasingly make their own choices about whom they see and what they do.

Through these years it's vitally important that we keep in touch with how they are feeling about themselves and about their place among their friends.

Stop & Think

Do you know where your teenager finds the most pressure – at school, youth group, in the sports team, on the street?

Where do they come in the pecking order?

Do they feel that they have to work hard to be accepted among their peers?

Think of the way your teenager introduces their friends to you. How do they behave with them when you are around? Are they embarrassed and evasive or at ease and natural?

Is there space somewhere in the home for them to hang out together?

Do they feel you like or dislike their friends? Why? How much do you see of them?

TYPICAL TEENAGE SCENES

1. My teenagers have to be at school by 8.30 am. They are always leaving things until the last minute, and something usually goes missing. They invariably end up asking me for a lift, as they've missed the bus and will get a late mark. What can I do to organise our mornings better?

2. I've tried to encourage my 14-year-old son to bring friends home with him. He won't. I really want to meet his friends and know more about whom he's hanging out with. How can I make this happen?

3. During a heated discussion with our teenage daughter, my husband told her that she couldn't go to a party that I know she's been looking forward to for weeks. I feel this was over-hasty, but I don't want to undermine his authority. How should we move forward?

FOLLOW-UP QUESTIONS

- How can you help your teenagers resist negative peer pressure?
- How can you prevent the same old things causing friction in the home, time and time again?

RE-CAP

In this chapter:

- We've considered how to set positive, healthy boundaries for our teenagers.

- We've outlined some of the areas of conflict, and given some guidelines on how to face issues together, distinguishing the important from the unimportant.
- We've recognised the ongoing pressure from their contemporaries.

TAKING IT FURTHER

Think of one aspect of your teenager's behaviour that upsets you regularly, and plan to do the opposite to what you normally do.

Begin by making a small change rather than a major one, the more specific the better. Set yourself realistic goals. For example:

- You're always getting drawn into and wound up by the petty squabbles between two of your children, so decide instead to leave them to sort things out themselves.
- You've got into the habit of shouting, so say to yourself, 'I'll only yell at them five times today instead of ten!'
- You find yourself constantly criticising the way they dress, so instead of making negative comments make yourself compliment them on just one thing.

Chapter 5
SECURITY, SEX AND SUBSTANCES
Teenage Issues

In this chapter, we will be tackling some of the big issues to help teenagers face the world in which they are emerging as adults.

As we start, here's another glimpse into the minds of our teenagers – a few more genuine questions and answers from some exam papers:

Q: What happens to your body when you age?
A: When you get old, so do your bowels and you get intercontinental.

Q: What happens to a boy when he reaches puberty?
A: He says goodbye to his boyhood and looks forward to adultery.

Q: Name a major disease associated with cigarettes.
A: Premature death.

Q: What is artificial insemination?
A: When the farmer does it to the bull instead of the cow.

Q: What is the most common form of birth control?
A: Most people prevent contraception by wearing a condominium.

HEALTH ISSUES

Bible View:

There is a right ownership of responsibility for our bodies, but the right isn't totally ours – it's a delegated responsibility. We're to look after our bodies precisely because they are not ours to do what we like with.

'Do you not know that your body is a temple of the Holy Spirit, who is in you, whom you have received from God? You are not your own; you were bought at a price. Therefore honour God with your body' (1 Corinthians 6:19–20).

EATING DISORDERS

When talking about eating disorders we often focus almost entirely on girls, but we must realise that boys are becoming increasingly aware of the emphasis on the 'perfect body'. There is a growing pressure on teenage boys to develop an impressive physique – a bulging 'six-pack' and muscular biceps – and most boys, particularly those who are late developers, worry about their height.

Dr Kate Middleton reports that '90% of teenage girls say that they hate their body'. Recent studies reveal that as many as a quarter of young teenage girls may have some kind of eating disorder, and that by the age of 13 around two-thirds of girls have already been on a diet.

Dieting is very common among teenagers (especially girls), and it can be quite hard to distinguish between those at genuine risk from eating disorders and those who are just dieting and showing the weight obsession typical of their age. However, on the whole a parent's instincts tend to be correct, so if you are concerned don't ignore the signs.

Here are particular warning signs to watch out for:

- Obsessive behaviour. Are they constantly reading books or articles on dieting, or checking food labels for their fat or calorie content?

- A desire to control. This may show itself in their developing a strict list of 'forbidden' foods, allowing themselves to eat only a very narrow or 'safe' set of foods and showing very little flexibility in their diet. They may also show signs of distress or panic if they are in a situation where they might have to eat food that is not on their 'safe' list.
- Isolation. They might develop a habit of eating alone or out of sight of others. You may notice that they are finding it increasingly hard to sit down with the family or with others to eat a meal.
- A tendency to deceive. For example, they might say they've already eaten when offered a meal, or that they're still full from something they've eaten earlier.
- A hint of neurosis, perhaps often complaining of feeling 'bloated'.
- Secrecy. You might find hidden food or stashes of food wrappers in their room.
- Excessive behaviour – perhaps frequent exercising. This again may well be done in secret, perhaps before you get up in the morning or after you go to bed at night.
- Binge-eating. You might realise that food is inexplicably disappearing from the kitchen.

Any combination of these may indicate an unhealthy relationship with food. So what can you do as a parent if you feel things are moving out of control?

We would suggest that you don't wait too long before addressing the issue. By the time you've noticed something is wrong, these habits may already have rooted themselves quite deeply.

Try to get alongside them and ask them what would be helpful. Remember it's better to focus on how they are *feeling*, not just on what they are or are not *eating*. Show them you want to understand their struggle, so talk to them about how they are feeling about themselves. Find out how they are coping with life rather than just how much weight they're putting on.

Bear in mind particular current pressures on them, such as exams, relationships or bullying, and try to help them make their own choices. You can make suggestions, but the decisions must come from them. So attempt to give affirmation without overwhelming them. Show them that you want to work together with them – maybe read up about the issues in books or on websites.

And here are some ideas of what *not* to do as a parent:

- Don't say or do nothing – it implies that either you're frightened or you don't care.
- Don't let your shock or fear show more than your concern. You may well be worried, but they have enough worries of their own without hearing yours as well.
- Don't expect them to pull themselves together and eat normally.
- Don't try to control their eating habits – it's actually better if you don't focus on food and weight too much with them.
- Don't condemn or judge them, or use emotional blackmail; for example, in your anxiety saying things like, 'Do you know what this is doing to me and the family?'
- Don't expose them by telling lots of people unnecessarily. They will be more aware than you realise about the conversations you're having about them, so respect their privacy.

Eating disorders are just one health issue, but they are an important one that often interacts with other health issues during the adolescent years.

LSD – LOVE, SEX AND DATING

Sex is everywhere, it seems. It's used to sell virtually any product, from washing powder to ice-cream to coffee. Sexually explicit lyrics are part and parcel of nearly every pop song our teenagers listen to, and early evening soaps have teenagers discussing not whether or not they should be 'doing it', but when, with whom and how often.

Our teenagers live in a world where they are constantly bombarded by other people's views on sex (says Steve Chalke in *Sex Matters*). Just listen to some of these quotes:

> 'Falling in love – how to know when you are ready to go all the way'
> 'Six steps to hot summer sex'
> 'Orgasms: a girl's guide to toe-curling, spine-tingling, back-arching bliss!'

Forget the top shelf. These are all genuine front-cover captions from best-selling magazines aimed at a young teenage market. And even if *your* teenager isn't buying them, you can bet that one of their friends is passing them around.

The pressure on them to think as other people think and do as other people do is enormous.

The pressure to do what they think all their friends are doing is intense – even when it turns out later that most of them aren't actually doing it at all. Most 15-year-olds are made to feel that they are the only virgins left on the face of the earth.

This is an excerpt from a letter in the *Daily Mirror* newspaper written by a young girl, explaining why she had sex for the first time:

> We started kissing and cuddling and one thing led to another. I had hoped it would be very special – you know, very romantic. I imagined that it would be something out of a film with music and flowers. Unfortunately it was over very quickly and I just thought: 'Is that it?'
>
> I was shocked that I had actually gone through with it and became very tearful. . . It sounds so obvious now but at the time I hadn't thought hard about it. Naively I just wanted to be part of the gang who had done it. The next day when I went to school my friends asked: 'Have you done it yet?' I pretended that it had been a great experience and they were very proud of me and made me feel part of the gang. But I felt as if I had done something wrong and in my heart I wished I hadn't gone through with it. But as far as my friends were concerned, I was now one of them.

And the pressure doesn't end there. A letter came through Emily's door during her first week at university with some free condoms inside and a note that said: 'Enough of this moralising – sleep with whoever you want, whenever you want, but do it carefully.' The message she was being given at one of the most vulnerable points in her life – just as she had left home – was that she not only could, but should, have any number of sexual partners, as long as she was careful. In other words, being responsible meant having 'safe sex' – as if sex can ever be safe outside of a relationship of mutual commitment and trust.

Rightly or wrongly, there's a real battle going on for our teenagers' minds. Teenagers are sponges, soaking up information and opinions from the world around them. If *you* are not influencing them, you are about the only person around them who isn't! Everyone else is doing it for you, but with *their* values and standards rather than yours.

Bible View:

The Bible tells us that 'sexual immorality' is every form of sexual relationship outside of the lifelong commitment of marriage. Treating other people with honour is a control that has to be learned. The New Testament says:

'It is God's will. . . that each of you should learn to control his own body in a way that is holy and honourable' (1 Thessalonians 4:3–4).

Sooner or later your son or daughter will make their own choices about when, where and with whom they have sex. But wouldn't it be tragic if, as they were making those choices, your child didn't know what you felt about one of life's most important issues, just because you were too embarrassed to talk or had never found the right moment?

So how do we talk to them? How can we best communicate our values and beliefs about this whole area of sex? Probably the first thing we all come to realise is that moralising doesn't work. It's much more effective to prompt our teenagers to think issues through for themselves.

We can help them do this mainly by asking questions and giving them opportunities to talk. Asking questions helps them to express their opinions and to set their own guidelines – ones that they're much more likely to respect and follow because they've thought them through themselves. They've not been imposed by their parents.

So you might initiate conversations with them by asking questions like:

- 'What advice would you give your younger brother or sister before going out on their first date?'
- 'How would you like to be treated on a date?'
- 'How would you answer if he said that you don't really love him if you don't want to have sex?'
- 'What do your friends say about sex?'

By asking these sorts of questions we are showing that we're interested in their opinions and that we don't think we have all the answers.

'Panic' is one of the words parents most use when describing their emotions as children hit adolescence. Here is a 'Don't Panic' list:

- Don't live in denial. Your child is growing up into an adult world and you must recognise and accept that transition.
- Don't draw too much attention to the changes, particularly their bodily changes. Comments like 'What hairy legs you've got' and 'Is that a moustache appearing on your upper lip?' are not entirely helpful (and that's just for the boys!).
- Don't show anxiety or foreboding. It's important that they feel you're looking forward to the changes that are happening.
- Don't deny their feelings. If they feel you only want the 'happy child', they may only try to connect with you when they're happy.
- Don't leave them to work out their own sexual standards and goals.
- Don't be taken unawares. Christine remembers as our eldest daughter, Emily, was going out of the door for her first teenage party, desperately giving in two minutes the two-hour talk she should have had months before!

Stop & Think

What are some of the things making you panic as your teenager hits puberty?

It may be good for us sometimes to admit our ignorance of the world they are growing up in and the very different pressures they face today. The most important thing is to keep the channels of communication open between us; to keep talking.

You may find this fact rather surprising, but most teenagers want to hear about sex first from their parents. As they grow through their teenage years we need to be able to talk with them, not just about what sex is (the nuts and bolts), but also about what we think and feel about sexual matters or issues. In Nicky and Sila Lee's words, 'the slow "drip-feed" method over the years is far more effective than the one Big Talk'.

We should be ready to talk to our teenagers on a whole range of topics:

- changes in body shape and size
- changes in hair, voice, skin and body odour
- sexual organs
- masturbation
- virginity
- pornography
- sexual attraction
- flirting/kissing/heavy petting
- the dangers of casual sex – physical and emotional.

So think through what you might say on these different topics. Do some research and be ready for the conversation. Don't feel that your job is over just because you've had 'The Talk'. We need to *keep* talking to our teenagers, taking the initiative as well as answering their questions.

Now we all know that this isn't easy. Talking about these things makes most of us feel foolish, embarrassed and inadequate. Most of *our* parents didn't do a very good job, and we're fairly sure we won't either. But let's believe that we can start a new tradition: the tradition of preparing our children properly for adolescence.

Take advantage of the little everyday opportunities that come along. For example, use the media. We noticed a very effective piece of education on sex in an episode of *Friends* when Rachel tells Ross that she's pregnant. He is so shocked he is speechless for about 30 seconds. Then he blurts out, 'But we used a condom!' Rachel patiently explains that condoms don't always work. Ross looks even more shocked and screams, 'They should say that on the box!'

It's important to keep talking but not to get too heavy or intense or long-winded. You'll just put them off getting themselves into a similar conversation again. Keep things casual. If you don't, they will.

One evening Paul took advantage of a 'boys only' kitchen supper to have a conversation with Max about sex. All was going well, and Paul thought they were just getting into the subject, when Max walked over to the fridge, opened the door and as he peered inside said rather profoundly, 'Well, the thing is – once you've lost your virginity you've lost it for ever. . . chocolate mousse or yoghurt?' and promptly ended the discussion.

Here are some suggestions of opening questions that you might consider using in different situations with your teenagers – when you're watching a TV programme or a film, reading a magazine article, or commenting on how people behave or dress:

- 'Why do you think TV and films rarely show sex that isn't perfect?'
- 'How can you tell the difference between lust and love? How do you know when "this is the one"?'
- 'What limits would you set in a relationship and why? How would you get over the embarrassment of talking about your limits with a boy or girlfriend?'

- 'Why do you think people ignore the dangers (emotional as well as physical) of casual sex?'
- 'What do you think makes marriage different from living together?'
- 'What makes a good relationship? What makes a bad one? What do you look for in a boy or girlfriend?'
- 'Do you think it's good to wait until you get married to have sex, or not? Why?'
- 'Do you think it's true that people's first experience of sex makes a big impression?'

Stop & Think

What have you found to be particularly effective in starting good conversations about sex with your own teenagers? And what have you found to be particularly ineffective?

Most people agree that sex education is much more than giving information. We're preparing our teenagers for life and helping to develop in them a growing sense of responsibility for their own well-being and that of those around them. So, for example, talking about values (such as the importance of friendship as opposed to physical intimacy with the opposite sex) can influence teenagers more than we may imagine.

Many teenagers are bewildered and confused by the different messages they are picking up. The problem is that although a teenager's body is old enough to have sex, their emotions often aren't. Many are being pushed into sexual relationships too quickly and are missing out on the vital friendship stage. Physical sex often prevents teenagers from getting to know each other and offers them an escape from reality into what they believe is 'instant intimacy'. They end up picking partners who look sexy and cool, when it's far more important for them to learn to talk and listen and have fun and make friends first.

We should be encouraging them to join youth clubs or sports groups so they can develop many different friendships. We can help too by making their friends welcome in our home – by giving them space to 'hang out' together. In our experience this has meant vacating the sitting room for an evening and letting them watch their film together, or allowing our store cupboards to be raided by hoards of teenage scavengers, or sacrificing our plans for an early night when they all come back after an evening out.

Our teenagers are facing more and more pressure at a younger age to be sexually active. Are we preparing them as best we can to cope with the pressure? Our job as parents is not just to present them with the facts of life, but to help them to work out clear practical guidelines as well. If we're just doing the first part we're only doing half the job.

We've got to get past our embarrassment and talk with our teenagers about these things, because not many others will talk with them in this way. But of course we must choose our moments wisely – we mustn't hound them or fall into the trap of over-doing it.

If we do, they'll quickly get suspicious and think we're either obsessed with sex or we don't trust them.

They may laugh at us now, and tell us how quaint and out of touch we are, but what we say may register with them and may profoundly affect their decisions in the years ahead. Our children have always laughed at a simple little motto we use about boy/girl relationships: 'If you haven't got it, don't touch it!' They may have laughed at it, but they've remembered it!

At the end of the day, it's our responsibility to do all we can to help our teenager make good sexual choices – ones they won't regret in the morning, or even five or ten years down the line. It's true, we can't make their choices for them, and if they disappoint us, we have to show we still love them. One friend of ours said that when she realised her teenage daughter was sleeping with her boyfriend, she found it very difficult to respond to her affectionately. But she had to get past that and somehow show that she still loved her. We can't control what they do any more. We can only act as a guide.

SAD – SMOKING, ALCOHOL AND DRUGS

DRUGS

The following quote is from Rob Parsons, *What Every Kid Wished Their Parents Knew* (Hodder & Stoughton 1999):

> Dave, aged 16:
> My Dad said: 'You've never seen any drugs, have you?'
>
> I knew that he just wanted me to say 'No, Dad' because then he'd feel safe and as if he had nothing to worry about. He likes everything to be cosy and manageable.
>
> Truth is, loads of kids in my school take them and I could get him anything he wants, so I told him so. He yelled at me then as if I was already

> facing death as an addict. I'm not, I've got too much sense. He didn't see that just knowing where to get it doesn't mean you are. He couldn't see that he should be glad that I've kept on the right side of it all and learnt how to deal with the pressure. He just gave me a whole load of don'ts and a rambling lecture. To be honest, most of what he said was so out-of-date and so incorrect anyway, it wouldn't have helped a bit.

Here are just some of the reasons why teenagers use drugs and alcohol:

- It makes them feel they belong
  – it takes away many of their inhibitions.
- It's fun
  – it's an easy source of pleasure.
- It's easily obtainable
  – 'you can get them anytime, anywhere'.
- It's the 'in' thing to do
  – it's just part of a night out.
- It fills the emptiness
  – feelings of worthlessness/loneliness disappear.
- It offers relief from internal pressures
  – it gives an immediate high.
- It's 'cool' to take risks
  – to rebel or shock.

Drugs are not a problem to young people – to them they are the answer to the problems of life. Whatever their need – boredom, fun, pain, emptiness – young people find that drugs work. Taking drugs provides a temporary answer. It gives them freedom, release, acceptance, a 'buzz'.

This is often the hardest thing for parents to understand or accept, but we must if we want to do something about the problem. The reason young people take drugs is because they work, and the immediate benefits outweigh the long-term risks. Most teenagers don't think a week ahead, let alone years!

Stop & Think

Do you think your teenager might be able to relate to any of these reasons now?

What is clear is that just to say 'no' – to say to our teenagers, 'Don't take drugs, whatever you do!' – is ineffective. It's not enough. There was an advertising campaign in the States that had the simple words *just say no*. It was shown not to work. It was inadequate. Apart from anything else, it invited the retort: why not *just say yes*?

There was a campaign in the UK as well. It was a picture of a junkie, aimed at putting off potential heroin-takers. But this junkie became a teenage pin-up. The advertising campaign had exactly the opposite effect to what was intended. Slogans are not enough to protect our teenagers. They need to understand 'why'. Young people need information and facts about drugs and alcohol to help them make their choices. But they need more than that: they need skills to help them make good choices.

Earlier we looked at how to help our teenagers cope with peer pressure, how to build up their self-esteem and make them feel secure and loved. These are all vital in equipping them to face the pressures around them.

The facts show that the majority of addicts were first introduced to drugs by their friends. We're not usually talking about someone 'out there' doing it *to* them. They are much more likely to have been passed on quite casually by a friend at a party. At this point, if they haven't thought through what they believe and why, they are much more vulnerable to the offer. We as parents can play an important part in helping them to make their own decisions and resist the pressure from others.

So here are eight tips on talking with your teenagers about drugs and alcohol:

1. First, ask questions. They probably know more than you think. We remember a particularly revealing conversation with our teenagers over the supper table one evening. We suddenly became much more aware of the world they were growing up in, and how streetwise our three 'innocent' children were. We learned more in that evening about their world and how they understood it than we had ever done before.
2. Listen carefully to what they have to say. Be willing to hear something new. Our three teenagers loved showing off the fact that they knew all the street names of the various drugs. Our ignorance encouraged them to show off their knowledge – they felt they were keeping us up to date! But it was actually a very useful exercise in finding out how much they knew.
3. Encourage them to talk about their feelings, not just their experiences.
4. Try not to resort to ignorant threats out of fear; for example, 'Ecstasy kills.'
5. Talk with them about making choices. Encourage them to have their own opinions.
6. Think about the messages and attitudes you are passing on to your teenagers.
7. Don't be afraid of creating rules and boundaries, particularly about what happens in your own home.
8. Understand that sometimes teenagers just like to be contrary. They will enjoy making outrageous comments and seeing the effect they have on you.

Stop & Think

What has been your experience in talking with your teenagers? Which of these suggestions have you already implemented? Which of these do you feel you need to work on?

Have you thought through what your reaction might be if you found your child regularly smoked, or if you found drugs in their room, or if they came back drunk from a party? It's a very unusual family that doesn't find at least one of their children experimenting at some time during their teenage years. It's so important not to over-react. Remember that many of these experiences are experiments rather than lifestyle choices.

In all this, one of the hardest things as parents is to know when and what to share with our children. When to start talking about drugs will vary from family to family, but the right time is nearly always earlier than we think or would like it to be.

We can start talking about drugs in a very natural way with children who are still in primary school. For example, when they see you taking medicine you can talk to them about the positive side of drugs. At the same time you could begin to explain the harmful side if drugs are misused in any way. As they get older, if the subject of drugs or alcohol is mentioned on TV or in the newspaper, use the opportunity to ask them what they think.

When they reach secondary school, ask them what is covered in their drug education lessons, or what the school rules are about drugs and alcohol. Do they think they are good rules? At some point early on, tell them that if anyone – a classmate or a brother of a classmate – offers them something that looks like a sweet but isn't, first not to accept it, and secondly to come and tell you. Reassure them that no matter what they tell you, you won't be shocked or cross (both of which you may feel inside). It's essential that they know there is always a channel of communication open. Close this channel down and you won't know what is going on in the playground or at friends' houses.

We also need to be aware of the vulnerable moments in our teenagers' lives – such as when moving to a new school, finding a new set of friends, coming up to exams, moving to a new area, or witnessing their parents' marital difficulties – because that's when they might be more open to the pressure to take drugs.

Stop & Think

Have you talked with your teenager about drugs? How have they responded? And what have you learned?

What if we think our teenager is taking drugs?

Obviously we all hope that our teenagers will never take drugs, but if we are worried that they might be, what are the signs we need to recognise? Emotional signs are often difficult to pinpoint in the general rollercoaster of teenage life, but these are some of the signs to look out for with particular drugs:

- Stimulants (such as Ecstasy, poppers, speed or cocaine) excite the user. So watch out for significant changes in sleeping patterns, bursts of energy and then periods where they seem overtired for no apparent reason.
- Hallucinogens (such as cannabis, ketamine or magic mushrooms) heighten experiences in the short term – music becomes enhanced, jokes are funnier, emotions are more overwhelming – but in the long term these drugs will make the user paranoid and moody.
- Depressants (such as gases, glues and aerosols) slow down the heart rate, often making the user sleepy, possibly causing them to have slurred speech. There is a loss of inhibitions and a numbing of the emotions.

Now you see why these signs are really difficult to separate from normal teenage behaviour!

Physical signs can be more obvious:

- Eating habits become very erratic.
- Their appearance shows signs of change.
- They become more secretive and moody.
- They lose the ability to cope with school work or lose interest in hobbies.
- Money goes missing from your purse.

Most parents panic and become very emotional if they suspect their child is using drugs. But we need to try and keep a handle on our emotions, as these are the times when our teenagers need us the most and they need us to be calm and strong.

So try not to accuse your teenager – this will only start a row, and if you're wrong, you will damage your relationship. Try not to discuss things while they are under the influence of drugs or alcohol. This may sound rather obvious but it's important to choose a calm moment so that things don't just escalate out of control.

In the same way, try not to get angry or simply threaten with punishment. One of the most important things is to talk together and keep the relationship strong. You can still be firm about what behaviour is acceptable, particularly in the home if they are still living with you, but you must try to let them make their own choices and accept the consequences of their actions.

You can't make decisions for your teenagers – you need to let that responsibility go. Part of being a parent is to let our children make mistakes. The hard part is to try to protect them from making big mistakes that will harm them.

DRINKING AND SMOKING

So far we've focused mainly on abuse of illegal drugs in this section, but of course two of the most important drugs we need to worry about are nicotine and alcohol. Many sources say that drinking is an even bigger problem for teenagers today than illegal drug-taking. Alcohol abuse kills more people than all the other illegal drugs put together and smoking even more. Our teenagers are surrounded by alcohol. It's part of most recreational activity, so we need to help them to learn how to handle it carefully.

But what are they learning from us? Do they see us coming home from work and reaching for a glass of wine or beer to unwind? Do they see us coming home from an evening out having had slightly too much to drink?

Our teenagers watch us and learn from us, and they'll copy us. So how can we help them develop a responsible attitude towards alcohol?

We would suggest that you introduce them to alcohol, usually beer or wine, at home over a meal. Take away the mystery factor. Help them to learn not to drink it too quickly, to treat it with respect – it's not Coca-Cola. When your teenager starts going to parties, encourage them to stick to lower-strength brands, or to drink 'long' drinks. You could show them that even a seemingly innocent 'alcopop' contains a double measure of spirits. This surprises most teenagers, as these drinks are often disguised in a seemingly innocent looking bottle which looks more like a harmless fizzy drink than alcohol. Tell them to look out for each other and to notice if someone has had too much to drink.

We must realise that they will often learn from their own mistakes (just as we have) and we must allow them to do that. One of our teenagers drank too much on the last night of a holiday we were taking with some other families. It was their first experience of mixing drinks and they were very sick all night, and even on the journey home the next morning we had to keep stopping the car as they were still feeling ill. But the point was, we didn't need to say very much, as they kept saying, 'This is awful – I feel dreadful. I'm so sorry. I'm never going to do this again!' We must allow them to learn from their own mistakes.

It's wise not to be too heavy-handed about it all. We remember picking up Max from a party and realising as he got into the car that he'd had just a little too much to drink. He got home and promptly fell fast asleep fully clothed on our bed. We said nothing, but it's become a family joke that the next day he admitted to one of his sisters, 'Had a little too much to drink last night, but it's all right, the rentals [parents] didn't notice!'

If you are ever brave enough to hold a teenage party at home, make it clear that you will be around or close at hand. We are astonished at how many parents leave teenagers to party on their own. Remove temptations such as your own stock of drink (especially spirits), and have plenty of starchy food available – bread, rice and pasta, for example. Allowing them to drink on an empty stomach is just asking for trouble, so encourage them to eat something during the evening. Work out an end time to the party, and discuss with your teenager how this will happen. It also might be kind to warn the neighbours!

Our first experience of a proper teenage party in our house was disastrous, and most of it was our fault. Emily had arranged to meet friends for her 17th birthday celebration at a bar near our house, and she asked if a number of them could meet up at the house first. So girls started arriving at around 8 pm, and went up to her bedroom at the top of the house, where there was also a spare room. Before we knew it, more and more youngsters (male and female) had made their way upstairs, the music was turned up and 'refreshments' appeared.

We began to enquire when they were planning to move off to the bar, and were assured that they were all going very soon. But time went on and it became obvious that they were all very happy staying put in the top two bedrooms of our house. They were all being so good natured about it that we let things go on, not wanting to spoil things for our daughter on her birthday. But we were totally unprepared for this scenario. Having thought the party was being held in a bar, we'd set no ground rules (such as bedrooms being 'out-of-bounds') and so the party went on into the early hours.

We finally found ourselves in a ridiculous situation. Having gone to bed, we realised that we would have to get dressed again (you're always at a slight disadvantage trying to take firm parental control in your pyjamas!) to go and suggest that the party come to an end. We wouldn't make that mistake again in a hurry.

TYPICAL TEENAGE SCENES

1. I do a school run with a group of my son's school friends a couple of times a week. My 13-year-old son has been openly talking with them about 'dating and dumping' girls. There is a lot of joking and boasting, and I realise most of it is sheer bravado, but I'm concerned that if I don't say anything he may assume that I approve of the way they are talking. I don't want to come across heavy-handed. What should I do?

2. My 16-year-old daughter has been going out with a boy from her school for six months. She recently told us that they have started sleeping together, and that his parents allow this to happen when she stays over at their house. We are horrified. She doesn't want us to talk to the boy's parents, but we feel that we must. We don't want to go behind her back. What should we do?

3. My 13-year-old girl has started to read various teenage magazines. The problem pages in these magazines lay a lot of emphasis on how to give pleasure in a sexual relationship. I am uncomfortable with this. Is this something I should talk to my daughter about?

4. I feel differently about my son experimenting with sex from the way I feel about my daughter. Am I being inconsistent?

FOLLOW-UP QUESTION

In what ways do you personally feel challenged to review your own lifestyle choices and to talk more openly about any of these issues?

RE-CAP

In this chapter:

- We've thought through some of the various disorders, physical and mental, and explored some of the signs to watch out for.
- We've tried to facilitate good, open conversations about our teenagers' relationships, and the whirlwind of emotions surrounding these.
- We've explored the whole area of substance abuse, dependence and addiction.

TAKING IT FURTHER

- Look back at the suggested questions for opening up topics of conversation with your teenagers. Think how you personally might answer some of these questions yourself.
- Choose one or two of the questions and try to open up a discussion with your teenager this week.

Chapter 6
CONSUMERISM, CASH AND CYBERSPACE
Teenage Pressures

In this final chapter we will be tackling some more of the big issues, to help teenagers face the world in which they are emerging as adults.

MEDIA AND CONSUMERISM

Bible View:

Helping our teenagers to handle money, material goods, other people's things and the advertising pressure that undermines good sense is one of the most important skills we can instil in them. Jesus said:

'Whoever can be trusted with very little can also be trusted with much, and whoever is dishonest with very little will also be dishonest with much' (Luke 16:10–11).

Our teenagers are told that they are defined by outward signs: you are the labels you wear, the car you drive, your body size/shape, the level of popularity you have. You are even the toothpaste/shampoo that you use! As one teenager said, 'Take away my mobile phone and you take away a part of me!'

How do we keep the obsession with mobiles, gadgets, clothes and designer-wear under control? It's important for us to grasp that clothes for teenagers are as much about belonging as about acquiring the actual items. Clothes are a very powerful way of showing that you belong to your chosen group.

For girls in particular, shopping can seem like a major hobby (if not an obsession), taking up hours of their time. But what we must realise is that shopping to them is a communal activity. It's as much about socialising with their peers and affirming their place in a group as about buying things.

Stop & Think

What is most important to your teenager? Quantity of clothes? Exclusive brand names/designer-wear? Gadgets, such as mobile phone, mp3 player? Who or what influences their choices?

Maybe it would be appropriate at this point to ask ourselves if we have passed on our 'designer desire' to our teenagers. Do we covet all the latest gadgets, high-spec cars and expensive labels?

You might find the following suggestions helpful in dealing with your teenagers as consumers.

- Decide on a certain amount of money together *before* you go out shopping with them. This should help you not to be pressurised into buying things on the spur of the moment. One helpful hint is, rather than taking cards, take cash instead. Or give them a certain amount of cash and let them see how much they can buy with it. Then they will really feel its worth.
- Talk about the things you or your teen could buy with the extra money required for designer labels. They may be quite shocked about how much more a label costs.
- Explore cut-price solutions in designer outlets. Check out the treasures to be found in charity shops. Vintage from a car boot sale can be more chic than a brand-new label, and it's unique.
- Show them that you want to be generous. Come towards them, but show them also that we have a responsibility as consumers. Were our clothes made with child slave labour or were they fair-traded? Are they environmentally friendly? Many of our teenagers have high ideals on these issues and may well be the ones to challenge us.
- Be more open with them about the pressures on the family budget – allow them to see the bigger picture. You don't have to go into great details – just explain what money is coming in and how it goes out. Treat them in a more adult way. We've found that our children have always responded very sensitively when we've talked through with them what we can and can't afford. So often it's shown them that we'd love to give them the things they're longing for. It's not that we don't *want* to – it's just that sometimes we can't.
- Try to be positive about the choices they make. Their clothes are an expression of themselves, so compliment them. Don't knock their pleasure. Our two daughters have very different styles of

dress. Emily's style is very similar to Christine's, so it's very easy for Christine to shop with her and to appreciate what she chooses. Julia has a style all of her own and it's often been hard to agree on 'what is appropriate' (which is, according to the girls, a favourite phrase of Christine's). It's particularly hard when it's your money that you feel is being used on yet another outrageous outfit. But over the years it's been important to step back and allow Julia to make her own statement, and to admire her individuality.

Stop & Think

How could you encourage your teenager to make sensible choices without seeming mean or controlling?

MONEY AND DEBT

Bible View:

Debt is fast becoming one of the greatest social problems in this country. It's better to warn about the dangers of debt, and give helpful training in how to handle money before there is even the opportunity to handle a plastic card. The book of Proverbs is full of advice about money and debt:

'. . .if you lack the means to pay, your very bed will be snatched from under you' (Proverbs 22:27).

While they're still living at home, we would advise working out a basic monthly allowance with your children and giving them freedom to spend it as they want. Even a 5-year-old given 50p to spend at the corner shop will resent it if you try to dictate how it's spent. A teenager told how to spend their allowance will naturally react in just the same way (as you might if your boss told you how to spend your salary). It's better to give guidance on how an allowance is to be spent *before* you give the money rather than afterwards. For example, you can say, 'I don't expect this money to be used on alcohol or cigarettes.' But the basic principle is: once given, the allowance is theirs and we must let them make their own decisions – and their own mistakes.

It's good, of course, to take an interest in what they buy and to encourage them to save up for things they really want. We also need to resist the temptation to add to it on demand. Teenagers can be very persuasive when they want something, but we mustn't let them manipulate us just because they've made some wrong choices.

Our three have all handled money in very different ways. One of them is the spender, one is the hoarder and one is the generous one, who will always be ready with a handout.

Stop & Think

What would you consider to be a reasonable monthly allowance for a 16-year-old? How are you helping your teenager to budget?

Here are four tips to help us develop a strategy for passing on a responsible attitude for handling money.

Train them

Teenagers, you might have noticed, are somewhat self-obsessed and sometimes need a gentle reminder about the value of money and the realities of life. So don't be afraid to assess their finances with them. Have they a gap year to pay for or college fees to consider?

Before A-levels start biting into their free time, help your teenagers to get into an independent frame of mind by learning to pay their own way for some things.

Supermarkets pay several pounds an hour for 16-year-old 'ambient replenishers' (shelf-stackers to you and me). Unless they are falling behind at school, working within legal guidelines is unlikely to cause problems and can teach responsibility.

All of our teenagers have found local babysitting jobs from the age of 16. In fact the rates are so attractive we've often been tempted to do some moonlighting ourselves! It's certainly been a lovely way of getting to know other families nearby and our teenagers have often been able to do their school work at the same time (and watch everyone else's Sky TV).

As we mentioned earlier, mobile phones have become an indispensable part of a teenager's attire. But what do you do when your teenager's mobile bills take on a life of their own? We need to help them to come up with an affordable solution. For example, could they rely more on SMS? If they have cheap internet access, how about sending messages from free SMS sites? Pay-As-You-Go guards the expenditure and can be one of the best alternatives when they're younger.

Teach them

You can't always get what you want and the lesson our teenagers need to learn is not to acquire something if they can't afford it. This is especially important to learn in these days of easy credit.

One day soon, your teenager will be earning and managing their own budget, but right now you have to foot the bill. So start now with a problem-solving approach when spending issues arise. Rather than just getting into arguments, encourage them to discuss and solve their own problems with your help. In this way, you are giving them increasing control and responsibility and are starting a dialogue that will be invaluable through the next few years as they push for more independence.

Before they leave home, consider letting them manage their own budget for a trial period. Give them the total amount available for clothes, pocket money and expenses over a specified time, and then let them decide how to spend it. Give them a book to keep track of costs – and keep an eye on them!

When Emily went off to university and was obviously going to be managing her money completely on her own, we made a suggestion that she found quite helpful. We suggested that it would be easier for her to keep a check on what she was spending if she took out £50 cash at the beginning of each week, rather than constantly using her credit card. She found that helped her know how quickly money was being spent and stopped her from over-spending without realising.

Warn them

Banks love students – they're the high earners of tomorrow. But it's important for students to be discriminating when choosing an account. Most banks are very keen to offer students credit cards, but think carefully before encouraging your teenager to accept them. Remember to take into account the interest payable and the penalty fees for missed payments. It's also worth considering your teenager's ability to resist temptation when funds are running low.

All banks offer freebies, but how worthwhile are they? In most cases, a student railcard will be much more valuable than CD vouchers.

One of our teenagers ran up a horrendous mobile phone bill while they were abroad, not realising the extra charges. We thought it should have been obvious, but we also realised that we maybe should have been quicker to warn them.

Protect them

The world we live in very quickly teaches our young people that it's OK to be in debt. Banks offer overdraft facilities with little thought to how a teenager can make repayments. Student loans put them into debt that they often find impossible to repay for many years. And what it teaches them, quite subtly, from a very young age, is that it doesn't matter if you're living off money that isn't yours.

Soon after Julia opened an account, she went overdrawn by a small amount. Because she didn't pick up on it very quickly, the bank charges ended up being way more than the overdraft. We realised that we should have given her a little more instruction and also protected her from such a situation by suggesting she open a different sort of account.

Stop & Think

When do you think is the appropriate age for teenagers to handle cash cards/credit cards/store cards? What do you think they have picked up from watching how you spend money?

GITS – GAMES, INTERNET, TEXTING AND SURFING

The past few years have seen the introduction of a new area of teenage life where many parents have little knowledge of what's going on.

The internet and mobile technology play an increasingly important part in the lives of our young people – they've become part of their identity. Teenagers today have access to 24/7 entertainment, interaction and communication via the internet.

They are very easily drawn into spending hours and hours playing games, finding information and communicating with friends (and strangers) online, and there is a real risk that they can become so immersed in their online world that their virtual world can seem to take over their real world.

Essentially, anyone with access to the internet can become dependent on it, regardless of age or gender. And it's easy to see why. It's a very attractive world that is easily accessible; it offers continuous entertainment and stimulation with no demands or commitments.

It also offers the opportunity for anonymity and can provide a very attractive escape from reality. It becomes a secret place where inhibitions are lowered and an increased sense of intimacy is experienced – although of course we recognise this is a false intimacy.

So how can we as parents watch for the signs of it becoming an obsession, even an addiction, with our teenagers? Obsessive behaviour takes the form of particular activities and might include any or all of the following:

- Relationships – spending excessive amounts of time starting and maintaining online friendships in chat-rooms, which begin to replace real-life friends and family.
- Money – compulsively gambling online, trading online and taking part in online auctions.
- Information searching – compulsive web surfing or database searches.
- Gaming – obsessive computer game playing, including multi-user games.
- Sex – addiction to adult chat-rooms, cyber sex or pornography on the internet.

Researchers have argued that more than 20 hours per week constitutes internet addiction, although time is not the only indicator of this becoming a problem. Here are some other indicators that may help you decide if your teenager is spending too much time online:

- You notice a preoccupation with the internet. It seems to have become the strongest source of satisfaction in their lives.
- There seems to be increasingly less investment in relationships with friends. The internet begins to take precedence over other arrangements and commitments they have made.
- You may notice an increased emptiness, depression or irritability when they're not at the computer.
- There will often be a deception about the amount of time spent online.
- There may be lack of sleep through long and often late hours on the computer, again making them irritable and uncommunicative.
- There may be declining school results and a lack of interest in other activities.
- There will always be a denial of the seriousness of the problem.

'VIRTUAL REALITY'

Stop & Think

Have you discerned any signs of vulnerability in your teenager in the ways described above? Do you think you need to address any of these points?

If you are concerned about the effect internet use is having on your teenager, don't leave it too late. Be watchful and take it seriously. Just because it's in the home doesn't mean they are safe. Try to avoid computers in bedrooms – move the computer into a shared family room. This should be a basic rule in every family home. If computers are left in your children's rooms, they have the freedom and privacy to go online when they want and where they want. Instead, position them in shared rooms where you can easily keep an eye on things without it looking as though you're 'spying' on them.

Keep everything out in the open. If you are worried, try to find out how much time they really are spending online. It's all too easy in a busy household to be unaware of how long your children are spending on the computer (or on the TV or phone for that matter). Without being heavy-handed we can encourage some healthy patterns, particularly on school nights.

Try to work out some ground rules. Don't ban the internet – that will only make them mad! Instead, work out where they go online. What are the regular sites they go onto? Have an agreed 'internet time' – limiting the amount of time they spend online each day. Perhaps you can agree on no surfing or instant messaging until they complete their homework. Work out a policy to limit access to chat rooms, and certainly get agreement that they will never give out their name, mobile number or address to strangers.

You could maybe explain it to them like this – they would never dream of walking down the street with a placard hung round their neck giving that information! But that is exactly what they're doing when they release those details in certain places over the internet. Paedophile rings are known to swap their lists of children's names and addresses gathered from chat rooms over the internet. We must make sure our teenagers understand the dangers.

Try talking to them about why they're spending so much time online. If you can, encourage them to participate in other activities, particularly physical ones. Maybe find an offline activity that links in with their online interest – for example, kicking a football around rather than playing computer football games all the time. And if you suspect things are getting really out of hand, consider speaking to their teacher, or the school's counsellor, or a youth leader.

Bible View:

The Bible warns us against loving material things because they can become idols:

'Do not love the world or anything in the world' (1 John 2:15–16).

An idol is rarely a bad thing in itself, but rather a good thing in the wrong place in our longing and affection, leading to obsessive habits, possessive ownership and compulsive use. Ultimately, idolatry is worship of the created goods of this world rather than of the good Creator, who alone can bring these things under control.

TYPICAL TEENAGE SCENES

1. My 14-year-old daughter seems to have no hobbies or interests at all; just a circle of friends she spends all her time with, reading teenage magazines, trying out make-up and swapping clothes. The frivolity of this gets me down. What can I do to encourage more constructive use of her time?

2. My 15-year-old son is addicted to computer games. He seems to want to do nothing else and I can't bear the violence of the games he chooses. What can I do?

3. I'm worried that my 16-year-old daughter is going into chat-rooms and making contact with unknown characters. She is becoming more withdrawn and secretive, turning off the computer when I enter the room. I have also just realised how late she is staying online at night. She dismisses my attempts to talk to her about this and says I'm being paranoid. What should I do?

FOLLOW-UP QUESTIONS

- Should we pay our teenagers to baby-sit for their younger siblings?
- Is it wrong to offer money incentives for passing exams?

RE-CAP

In this chapter:

- We've considered the tremendous pressure of advertising and the media on this very self-conscious group in society, for whom 'image' is everything in clothes, music and electronic gizmos.
- We've looked at the stress caused by the first handling, and mishandling, of money in a debt culture – and the subtle pressure of gambling.
- We've tried to uncover the secretive world of internet chat-rooms, virtual reality, and the increasingly absorbing problems of web-surfing, computer games and pornography, including mobile phones and texting.

TAKING IT FURTHER

Think of six things that have particularly struck you while reading this book and decide how you are going to put them into action with your teenagers. We would encourage you to be as practical as possible. So, for example, instead of saying, 'I have been challenged to be more understanding towards my teenager,' pin it down by saying, 'I've been challenged to spend more regular time with my teenager, and I'm planning to go out for a coffee/pizza/burger with them once a fortnight.'

Or instead of, 'I've been challenged to be kinder to my teenager,' you could say, 'I realise that I've been losing my temper over too many things with my teenager recently, so I'm going to choose a moment to talk with them and apologise and work out a way forward.'

Commit yourself to some sort of action plan so that you can work on those things that have struck you as particularly important.

HOW TO RUN A *PARENTING TEENAGERS* COURSE

This book originated as a six-week course for parents of teenagers in our church. All the materials for running a course are available and we would encourage you to consider running a Parenting Teenagers course in your own church, school, home, or community centre. Here are some questions answered to help you run your own course.

What is Family Time?

Family Time is a collection of resources that provide tools, practical advice and support to parents. These resources come under two headings, Parenting Children (for families with under-twelve-year-olds) and Parenting Teenagers. This book is the sequel to the course on Parenting Children written by Mark and Lindsay Melluish, and both books have a course attached to them.

The Family Time courses present churches with a unique opportunity to build bridges into local communities and meet parents at their point of need. They're ideal for use in your local church, but we've tried to make the courses as adaptable and accessible as possible. They could go equally well in a children's centre or school or community centre, or in your own home – anywhere you can gather a group of parents together.

The aim is to empower parents to move from simply surviving family life to being proactive in leading families that are strong and healthy – families that seek to make a difference in the communities where they live.

Family Time is based on Christian principles, and aims to equip and envision every parent, whether Christian or not, to deal with the many issues they come up against in family life.

Why run a Family Time course?

We've found that many parents are surprisingly lacking in confidence when it comes to leading their family – this is particularly true when children hit the teenage years. These courses aim to be very practical – providing a whole range of exercises, 'to do' tasks and discussion points. We hope we have provided a resource that enables people to be equipped for the practical issues of parenting their children.

But more than that, this is a time to stop and reflect on your family life. As parents ourselves we recognise that so many of the things that we hope and dream for our children can be forgotten or lost in the pressures of everyday life. We hope to give parents the opportunity to remind themselves what is really important to them as they raise their children. Our aim is to equip parents to be a great source of strength and encouragement to their children.

Many people in our communities today are asking, 'How can we parent our children better?' Running a Family Time course can offer a first point of contact with people. Not only are they a great resource for parents, but they provide you with an opportunity to build relationship with your neighbours. They offer an opportunity to get involved – to meet people where they are.

This is also a place where parents can meet other parents. Parents of teenagers can often feel very isolated from each other – there's no more meeting other parents at the school gate or chatting together as you pick up your children from each other's homes. It's easy to feel rather detached from your teenagers' lives. By running a Family Time course, people make connections with each other again and your community is drawn back together.

What resources are available?

With all the resources that we now mention for this Parenting Teenagers course, there are a corresponding set for the Parenting

Children course. You can find out more about what is available and how to run a Family Time course by visiting our website www.family-time.co.uk.

There is a set of **DVD recordings** available which cover each of the six sessions in the Parenting Teenagers course. You can either use these to help familiarise yourself with the material as your prepare your own talks, or you could gather a group together and watch the DVDs instead of presenting the material yourself. There is also a promo DVD available that will give you a flavour of the course.

If you would like to teach the Parenting Teenagers course yourself, there is a full set of talk manuscripts available on downloadable pdf files. These can be found on the Family Time website (see above) and can be adapted to your own particular situation. We are very keen to make it as easy as possible for you to present the material yourself, so the **session notes** are written out in full for you to simply cut and paste on your own computer. We would really encourage you to make the material your own. We would particularly recommend that you put in your own examples of family life. You're very welcome to use the examples we give throughout the course, but as you get more familiar with the material it's so much better if the examples come from your own experience.

Each of your guests will also need a **course handbook** which is also published by David C Cook (UK). It's really essential for each of your guests to have one of these in order to follow the talks, fill in the exercises and make notes from what is taught. These handbooks contain the six sessions in note form, along with worksheets for your guests to fill in, and at the end of each chapter there are 'typical teenage scenarios' and follow-on questions for the discussion groups.

There are also suggestions for 'Taking it further' during the intervening weeks in their families. As in the book, we encourage the guests to begin working on the ideas that are presented at each session, by taking on the practical tasks suggested in 'Taking it further'. We've found this begins to put ideas and aspirations into action straight away. We also give them an opportunity to report on their experiences (good and bad!) each week.

There is a **PowerPoint presentation** to go with each session. There are also **A2 posters** to help you publicise your course, as well as **course invitations** which are supplied with a template so that you can overprint your own personal details. These are all available from New Wine Direct at www.newwinedirect.co.uk.

How long does the course last?

The Parenting Teenagers course involves six sessions which can be run consecutively, but most important is that you find the way that would best suit your group of parents. We've designed it so that each session stands on its own – so if you want you can use only two or three of them. For example, it would be easy to take the sessions on some of the big issues ('sex, drugs, alcohol and the internet') at any one time. We would encourage you to use the material imaginatively for your own situation.

Who should take part?

Ideally, where possible, we encourage both parents to do the course together – but we love it when those parenting on their own come too. We often link single parents up in the discussion groups with others in a similar situation, but not exclusively. When the exercises require people to turn and discuss, we recommend couples talk together, but we always make sure those parents who are on their own have someone (maybe one of the team) to turn to.

Who should speak and lead?

The main thing to realise when leading or speaking on a Family Time course is that you don't need to have the perfect family – which is a relief to most of us! You simply need to be someone who is willing to share their experiences (good and not so good!) and able to draw out and include others who are in different situations. It's important to keep emphasising that people are not expected to have all the answers and that you're all on a journey in parenting together. Everyone has something to offer and everyone is there to learn.

Before you begin the course you'll need to become familiar with the material. One way of doing this is to gather a small group of couples around you and do the course together in someone's sitting-room. Together you could work through the material and then branch out and run it as a larger course the next term. By then you will have spotted potential group leaders and they will have familiarised themselves with the content as well.

What is the format of a typical evening?

We usually begin with light refreshments at 7.30 pm – sometimes we offer soup and cheese for those coming straight from work, or simply a cold drink. We start the talk at 8.00 pm and try to finish promptly by the advertised time. Some people may want to stay and continue talking, but it's important to allow others to leave if they need to get home.

We find that a café-style set-up makes for a relaxed atmosphere – low tables with cloths, a candle, napkins and mugs ready for coffee and cake later on.

The first half of the evening consists of a certain amount spoken from the front but also a variety of exercises for people to do individually or in pairs. Keep a close eye on the time, particularly while people are doing these. We recommend that you give them no more than five minutes for each exercise. You may find that you have to keep stopping their conversations as you move on to the next section – but don't worry about this, simply encourage them to pick things up again with each other at another time.

At the end of the talk we break for refreshments (coffee and cakes) before going into discussion groups. This social time is crucial and should last about 20 minutes. It's a great opportunity for people to get to know one another and share stories, so make sure you leave time for it.

How do we organise the discussion groups?

We try to put people into groups who have teenagers of similar ages, as experiences vary enormously over the years. Try to keep these groups the same throughout the course so that people become familiar with each other's situations. Ideally we would have a maximum of eight to twelve people in a group. This gives plenty of opportunity to hear of others' experiences, while not being so large that it intimidates discussion.

What happens in the groups?

In Session 1 we would begin by asking the group to introduce themselves:

- names and ages of their children
- length of marriage if applicable
- occupation/interests
- what each person hopes to gain from the course, for them and their family.

It's important in this opening session to emphasise that everything said in the group must be **confidential**. This will make it feel a safe place in which people can open up without being afraid that the things they share will be spread further than the group.

You'll find the different scenarios at the end of each session in your handbooks for you to use in these group times. These are simply to open up discussion following on from the talk and to ground the teaching in real-life situations. There are also a number of follow-up questions, but we would encourage you to be flexible and not to feel that you have to work through the scenarios and questions strictly in order.

You might prefer to start the group time by simply asking, 'What struck you in the talk this evening?' or, 'What was the most important thing for you in tonight's talk?'

During the discussion groups the leaders should try to avoid doing all the talking – and especially avoid appearing to have all the answers. Their main job is to open up and facilitate discussion. Our experience is that by Week 3 you have to say very little because everybody on the course has something to share.

Also, don't be afraid to leave silences. Often people are preparing to say something and if we break the silence they may have lost that opportunity. This is the time in the evening when issues come out that are sometimes painful and need sensitivity.

Should we pray?

We close with prayer if appropriate. It's a good moment to ask for requests from the families in the group.

If your course is in a church, people will probably be expecting this. Prayer can take various forms – either open prayer all together, or splitting into threes and fours, or just one of the leaders praying for everyone – depending on the group make-up.

It may be that some groups don't start praying until Week 3 or 4, but we would encourage you to pray in your groups at some point in the course. Once prayer has been introduced then pray each week!

If your course is in a school or other neutral location, prayer might not be so comfortable. Some people may be expecting it, especially if they know that the church is running the course, but others may not. It's important to be sensitive and act accordingly.

How can we give ongoing support?

We think it's really important for people to be supported once the course is over. We try to encourage parents to link up and support one another. This often happens very naturally as people make new friends through doing the course together.

Many of the groups organise informal evenings together; or you could arrange a course reunion about three months after the course has finished. You could either take over a local restaurant for an evening or have a meal in someone's home to which everyone brings a contribution of food. It's a great evening for good food and a lot of fun.

The situation may arise where a family needs more in-depth help than you can offer as a church. Therefore it's really good to know of organisations locally where you can send people for more help.

Do we charge?

It's a good idea to make a nominal charge for doing the course. This tends to give people a sense of ownership and also enables you to provide guests with the Family Time handbook (and possibly the book) and coffee at no extra charge. We would suggest around £10–£20 per family.

What about resources?

It's well worth having a book table. To help you put this together there is a recommended booklist at the back of this book and in the handbooks. We tend to recommend a book each week and this encourages parents to read further on that particular subject.

A local Christian bookshop will normally supply books on a sale or return basis.

For more information

New Wine regularly holds Family Time seminars, either at their conferences or at other times of the year, to help people run these courses in their local churches and communities. Do have a look on the New Wine website for further information (www.new-wine.org), or if you have any more questions about Family Time please email info@family-time.co.uk.

We hope that if you have enjoyed and benefited from reading this book you will want to share this material. Why not consider running a course in your church or school, or simply gather some friends together in your home? We believe there is such value in working together and encouraging each other in our parenting, and that you will see the fruit of it in your family's lives and in your communities.

Here are a few quotes from parents who have attended a Parenting Teenagers course:

'It gave us fresh hope and motivation to reconnect with our teenager.'

'It was so encouraging to realise that we shared similar experiences with other parents of teenagers – we weren't the only ones!'

'The course allowed us to be "real" about our struggles.'

Recommended Books

Biddulph, Steve, *Raising Boys/Raising Girls,* Thorsons (HarperCollins) 1997.

Campbell, Ross, Kids in Danger, Chariot Victor (Cook) 1995.

Campbell, Ross, How to Really Love Your Teenager, Authentic Media 1999.

Chalke, Steve, The ParentTalk Guide to the Teenage Years, Hodder & Stoughton 1999.

Chapman, Gary, The Five Love Languages, Northfield Publishing (Moody) 2000.

Covey, Stephen, The Seven Habits of Highly Effective Families, Simon & Schuster 1998.

Dobson, James, Preparing for Adolescence, Kingsway Publications 1982.

Lee, Nicky & Sila, The Marriage Book, HTB Publications 2000.

Melluish, Mark & Lindsay, Family Time: Parenting Children, David C. Cook 2007.

Omartian, Stormie, The Power of a Praying Parent, Kingsway Publications 1996.

Parsons, Rob, The Sixty-Minute Father, Hodder & Stoughton 1995.

Parsons, Rob, The Sixty-Minute Mother, Hodder & Stoughton 2000.

Parsons, Rob, Teenagers – What every parent has to know, Hodder & Stoughton 2007.

Quinn, Michael & Terri, What Can the Parent of a Teenager Do? Family Caring Trust 1988.

Tripp, Paul David, Age of Opportunity, P & R Publishing 2001.

FAMILY TIME – PARENTING CHILDREN
THE BOOK

When we become parents we are entrusted with lives that we will inevitably mould and shape – both by what we do and by what we don't do. It is a privilege and a responsibility.

This book mines the wisdom that comes to us from the Bible, exploring in practical ways how we can raise our children within the framework of God's liberating, unconditional love – a love that

- seeks to build up
- tries to guide in right ways
- is not afraid to discipline when necessary
- does not demand performance
- always offers forgiveness.

'This is a splendid book for families everywhere: full of wise, thoughtful advice and practical ideas on the art of parenting that really work!'

Lyndon and Celia Bowring, CARE

'Bringing up children is a priority. Mark and Lindsay have provided a challenging and practical book on parenting. It will help us build good values into our children's lives.'

Mary Pytches

'Of all the books available on family life Mark and Lindsay's is the best I've read! They provide practical, biblical encouragement to all those seeking to make a good family great.'

Mike Breen

Mark and Lindsay Melluish have five children and live in London, where Mark is Vicar of St Paul's, Ealing. A course handbook and DVD are also available.